"Jacques Bidet has in recent decades carved out a distinctive theory of modernity that starts from, but strives to transcend Marx. In this lucid and wide-ranging book he develops this theory further by rethinking the project of democracy in the context of the accelerating ecological crisis that increasingly threatens humankind. This involves Bidet in both critically interrogating theorists and idéologues – including Lenin and Xi Jinping. Gramsci and Althusser, Laclau and Mouffe – and empirically exploring how political institutions, movements, and parties function in the contemporary world-system. The result is a book that both demands hard thinking and offers radical hope."

**Alex Callinicos**, *Emeritus Professor of European Studies, King's College London*

"Jacques Bidet incorporates essential elements of Marx's work and, at the same time, makes corrections, indicates blind points and opens up original paths. A call for an uprising of the Nation-World that unites class, race and gender and is guided by the compass of ecology. For us, in the continent of the Amazon Rainforest, inhabited by dozens of indigenous peoples and also of large urban concentrations, this original and exciting book adds a lot to the search for popular struggle."

**Armando Boito Júnior**, *Professor de Ciência Política, Editor of Critica Marxista*

# Can Common People Govern?

In *Can Common People Govern?*, the renowned French social theorist, philosopher, and historian Jacques Bidet offers a theoretical and political exploration of political parties, movements, and uprisings as forms of popular political organization. He highlights the contradictions of the party-form and the movement-form through a critical analysis of Lenin, Xi Jinping, Gramsci, Althusser, and the theorists of left-wing populism, Laclau and Mouffe. Popular political organization, he argues, must be related to the structure of modern society, in which the popular class is opposed in a "triangular duel" against a dominant class that includes two poles in conflictual connivance, "capital-power" and "competence-power" (or "elite"). This duality offers the common people an angle of attack for a risky alliance with this elite against capital. This class confrontation is put in the context of the ongoing ecological disaster and popular uprisings. In the age of disaster, environmentalism and social emancipation must be conceived as one and the same thing.

*Can Common People Govern?* is relevant to students of Marxism as well as wider readership interested in political thought and action.

**Jacques Bidet** is Emeritus Professor at the University of Paris-Nanterre, France, and the founder of the journal *Actuel Marx*. Since the 1980s, he has been developing a theory of modern society and history known as "metastructural theory of modernity." His work is mainly inspired by Marx and influenced by thinkers such as Althusser, Habermas, Bourdieu, Foucault, Wallerstein, and others.

## Marx and Marxisms: New Horizons

*Edited by Marcello Musto*

The peer-reviewed series *Marx and Marxisms: New Horizons* (edited by Marcello Musto, with Francesca Antonini as Assistant Editors) comprises rigorous scholarly books, accessible to general readers, that offer innovative and critical works in the field of Marx studies and Marxisms. The series publishes monographs, edited collections, and anthologies, by both prestigious and emerging international experts, in the fields of political theory, history of political thought, sociology, political philosophy, and heterodox economics. The books in this series provide original investigations within the Marxist tradition, push the boundaries of accepted interpretations and existing literatures, bring different concepts and thinkers into new relationships, and inspire significant conversations for today. They come from a wide range of academic disciplines, subject matters, political perspectives, cultural backgrounds, and geographical areas, producing an eclectic and informative collection that appeals to a diverse and international audience.

**Can Common People Govern?**
Political Parties, Movements, and Uprisings
*Jacques Bidet*

**Marxism in the Age of Ecological Catastrophe**
Theory and Praxis
*Eduardo Sá Barreto*

For more information about this series, please visit: www.routledge.com/Marx-and-Marxisms/book-series/MM

# Can Common People Govern?

## Political Parties, Movements, and Uprisings

**Jacques Bidet**

**Translated by Bradley Smith**

NEW YORK AND LONDON

First published 2025
by Routledge
605 Third Avenue, New York, NY 10158

and by Routledge
4 Park Square, Milton Park, Abingdon, Oxon, OX14 4RN

*Routledge is an imprint of the Taylor & Francis Group, an informa business*



*Library of Congress Cataloging-in-Publication Data*
Names: Bidet, Jacques, author.
Title: Can common people govern? : political parties, movements, and uprisings / Jacques Bidet ; translated by Bradley Thomas Smith.
Other titles: Classe populaire peut-elle gouverner? English
Description: New York, NY : Routledge, 2024. |
Series: Marx and Marxisms : new horizons |
Includes bibliographical references and index.
Identifiers: LCCN 2024030931 (print) | LCCN 2024030932 (ebook) |
ISBN 9781032843575 (hardback) | ISBN 9781003512356 (ebook)
Subjects: LCSH: Working class–Political activity. |
Social structure–Political aspects. | Social conflict–Political aspects.
Classification: LCC HD8031 .B5413 2024 (print) | LCC HD8031 (ebook) |
DDC 322/.2–dc23/eng/20240731
LC record available at https://lccn.loc.gov/2024030931
LC ebook record available at https://lccn.loc.gov/2024030932

ISBN: 978-1-032-84357-5 (hbk)
ISBN: 978-1-032-84359-9 (pbk)
ISBN: 978-1-003-51235-6 (ebk)

DOI: 10.4324/9781003512356

Typeset in Times New Roman
by Newgen Publishing UK

**To Annie, for her critical contribution to this book.**

# Contents

# Introduction

Across the globe, social and environmental movements have emerged that demonstrate peoples' capacity to resist neoliberalism's global power to dominate and destroy the planet. It remains to be seen how these movements might come together to form a lasting force. In *A Political Ecology of Common People*,[1] I portrayed the general disorder of the contemporary world. Here, I seek to formulate a pathway to a new world order—one based on popular political practice.

The question of political *practice*, of course, is inseparable from that of a political *program*, which involves designing institutions that enable popular political intervention. My question, however, is of a different order. It concerns *another dimension* of political practice, one that no one, as far as I can tell, has managed to tackle head-on, for lack of considering it to be a theoretical issue of *equal importance*. A program must address both the ecological disaster and the expectations of the popular masses, including those of the precarious and destitute, who exist in large numbers. However, these social-environmental demands must still be translated into a political practice capable of rallying the forces necessary to make them a reality. Today it seems that neither "parties" nor "movements," which compete for this role, meet these imperatives. It is therefore urgent to work on designing and implementing an alternative form of popular political coordination.

This implies—and in my view this is crucial—a critical reconsideration of a conviction that is more or less shared by the entire left: that the adversary to be defeated is "capitalism." In *Capital*, Marx proposes a vast historical fresco that describes how, as modern industry develops, *organizational* logic tends to prevail over the logic of the

DOI: 10.4324/9781003512356-1

*market*. Under these conditions, he believed that workers, "brought together and trained" by a more transparently collective form of work, would eventually be able to take control of this process and transform it into *cooperation* between "associated workers." Such was the great revolutionary utopia of the twentieth century. In the East, Lenin and his followers drew a radical conclusion: Society as a whole must become an organization. In the West, various arrangements were worked out that remained under the hegemony of capitalist markets. It seems to me that the left has never succeeded in deciphering the interplay of social forces that underlie, respectively, market-based and organizational forms of domination, nor in devising a political practice capable of leading us *to* a democratic order. In the spirit of today's attempts to "liberate work,"[2] I will therefore seek out a pathway to "liberate politics."

According to the general hypothesis developed in my earlier work,[3] which guides this book's approach to political strategy, popular political practice is a "triangular duel." It is certainly a *duel* because modern society comprises two classes. But it is paradoxically *triangular* because the dominant class itself comprises two poles. It seems to me that this hypothesis is realistic and very accessible to common sense. For a long time now, critical thinking has discerned, alongside capital-power, the existence of another power intertwined with it, the nature of which remains more difficult to identify. This idea appears in various forms and approaches that are more or less comparable with each other. It is sometimes called technocratic, bureaucratic, or administrative power; or the "technostructure"; or the "managerial class" (as opposed to the class of shareholders); or the "elite." It is also reflected in Foucault's concept of "knowledge-power" and Bourdieu's concept of "cultural capital." My analysis owes much to the theoretically revolutionary contributions of these two authors; but, as a critical heir to Marx, I integrate them into a broader conception of modern class structure. This leads me to argue that the other dominant power in contemporary society, in affinity and in tension with that of capitalist property, should be called "competence-power"—despite the reluctance this admittedly awkward choice of terminology may raise.

"Competence" is to be understood in the legal and political sense of competent authority. Therefore, it cannot be reduced to knowledge. It is rather a mixture of knowledge and non-knowledge. Outside of it, and confronting it, there are multiple forms of knowledge that are equally essential but do not confer the privilege of power. Because there is no more appropriate term, and despite the difficulties readers might initially encounter, I will therefore call the holders of competence the "competent." Their social *power* derives from the "competencies" they receive from a competent *authority*, for example, from a state issuing diplomas through public universities.

In themselves, these "competencies" do not confer more knowledge, but more power. Capital-power and competence-power interfere at all levels. However, they follow two distinct types of logic. Capital-power is exercised in the *market*, and competence-power, in *organizations* (in tasks involving "management" or "expertise"). I mean this in the generic sense that, beyond the possibilities of immediate cooperation through language, these are the two primary and constantly intertwined modes of rational coordination on a social scale. Thus, the dominant class is made up of both capitalists, who are endowed with property and privileges in the market; and the "competent," who are more numerous, more strictly hierarchized, endowed with privileges within organizations, and present as experts in a wide range of activities involving production, administration, education, health, justice, the army, etc. Standing in opposition to this class is the popular class—not a subordinate class, but a *fundamental* class, referred to here as "the common people." It is a class without privileges, yet endowed with social *power*, the contours of which we shall endeavor to reveal throughout this book. A "popular left" is one that is placed under the hegemony of common people.

Capital-power is certainly the *main adversary*, the public enemy number one, the great destroyer; however, for popular politics, the *main concern* is competence-power. If this is indeed the right approach to the problem, it is because popular political organization can only emerge on the condition that an *alliance* is built between common people and a defined fraction of the "competent," who have their own reasons for resisting capital. The competent, however, only consider such an alliance if it allows them to take the lead. Therefore, it is necessarily an alliance-*struggle*, a *struggle*-alliance, fraught with contradictions that make it essentially uncertain. This is the crucial problem of all popular politics, one that no "party" or "movement" can overcome. Such is the thesis that will be developed throughout this book.

The "triangular duel" between and within social classes takes place in the conditions of what has been called the "triptych of domination": *class-race-gender*. These are indeed the primary elements of a semantics and grammar of the social and environmental politics of common people. Methodologically, however, I will leave aside the question of gender, which presupposes a broader set of concepts than the one engaged here. Furthermore, I will not speak of "race," but rather of its matrix, the "nation" and what I call "nation relations."[4] This *structural* analysis, which concerns class structure, automatically leads to a *systemic* analysis of the system of nations and the world-system. The relations between "structures" and "systems" play out through the process of "nation-states." The history of modern political parties and movements, and the question of what national and global alternatives are conceivable today in the age of disaster, must be considered from this starting point.

We know that the great historical parties that set out to abolish capitalist power emerged in very diverse historical circumstances and contexts, and that they have had very different fates. On the one hand, there is the one-party model, which subordinates common people to the competent, as can be seen, albeit to different degrees, in the cases of Lenin and Xi Jinping (Chapter 1). On the other hand, in Western conditions, there is what I call the "party-among-others" model, which has slowly become impotent. From the outset, discerning the identity of competence-power has proven difficult. This epistemological obstacle is perpetuated in today's left-wing imaginaries, well beyond the virtual disappearance of communist parties. Evoking these outdated models will allow us to better understand what the left is hiding from itself (Chapter 2).

Faced with the obsolescence of the "party-form," a "movement-form" has emerged over the past few decades, particularly in southern Europe. Abandoning class analyses, this model has set itself the task of bringing together all popular aspirations and demands against a "ruling caste." A careful reading of the two masterminds of this doctrine, Ernest Laclau and Chantal Mouffe, will help us to better understand this approach, which refocuses politics on rhetoric and *leadership*, thus tending to mask the new strategies of competence-power. These two authors have certainly left the forefront of the debates. Their thesis according to which the social world is structured like a language has been definitively ruined by the powerful arguments that Bernard Lahire develops in his latest book.[5] However, we cannot avoid questioning the kinship between their *discourse* and the *practice* of left-wing populism, where the figure of the great leader is still asserted today, albeit in a paradoxical way (Chapter 3).

In what terms, then, should we conceive a strategy for human emancipation and the preservation of life? I have chosen to use the concepts of "triangular duel" and "triptych of emancipation." However, in the age of disaster, this approach only makes sense if the quest for emancipation manages to merge with the imperative of "survival," a term that expresses the powerful concept of sustaining life. I will therefore take up the "social-ecological hypothesis" of my previous work: environmental struggles and social struggles are strictly one and the same. This opens a pathway on which environmentalism is henceforth the compass of politics (Chapter 4).

We must still take stock of the social obstacles that stand in the way. Strategies to overcome them are necessarily specific to each national context and the multiple circumstances of the "here and now." We can, however, formulate a few more or less universal requirements to be met by any form of political organization of common people. On a global level, it is no longer a question of "organizing." The new International cannot be thought of as a coalition of revolutionary organizations, but only as a convergence of nations and multinational associations within a nationally diverse human community, to be built in the ecological form of the "world-nation." This concept calls for another one that is now essential, for the principle of solidarity it expresses concerns the entire world of living beings, all of whom share the same conditions of survival within the same habitat. It calls for a general "uprising" against the forms of domination that are destroying the planet, an uprising that will continue until the disaster is overcome and the final catastrophe averted (Chapter 5).

For the most part, this book adopts a global approach, confronting issues that have concerned humanity as a whole throughout the modern era. The case of France, analyzed through the twists and turns of its recent history, up to the time of this book's translation into English, completed in June 2024, is dealt with in the Appendix.

## Notes

1 Jacques Bidet, *A Political Ecology of Common People*, trans. David Broder (New York: Routledge, 2024). See this work for a systematic formulation of the theoretical framework that underlies the present book.

2 See, among others, Thomas Coutrot, *Libérer le travail* [The Liberation of Work] (Paris: Seuil, 2018); and Alexis Cukier, *Le Travail démocratique* [Democratizing Work] (Paris: PUF, 2017).

3 See Jacques Bidet, *Théorie générale: théorie du droit, de l'économie et de la politique* [General Theory: A Theory of Law, Economics, and Politics] (Paris: PUF, 1999); and Jacques Bidet, *L'État-monde: libéralisme, socialisme et communisme à l'échelle globale: refondation du marxisme* [The World-State: Liberalism, Socialism, and Communism on a Global Scale. Rebuilding Marxism] (Paris: PUF, 2011).

4 The expression "nation relations" is novel and somewhat jarring in English. The same goes for *rapport de nation* in French. It is unavoidable, however, because it is modeled on the expressions "class relations" and "gender relations" as the third element of the triptych of modernity. In each case, it is not only a question of the relations *between* classes, genders, or nations, but also of the relations between individuals and their class, gender, or nation; the other members of their class, gender, or nation; and the members of other classes, genders, or nations. Various facets are reflected and overdetermined in this concept, which is present in Marx's spirit, even if it does not exist in common Marxist literature. See Chapter 4 in this book and Bidet, *A Political Ecology of Common People*, Chapters 2 and 3.

5 See Bernard Lahire, *Les structures fondamentales des sociétés humaines* [The Fundamental Structures of Human Societies] (Paris: La Découverte, 2023).

## References

Bidet, Jacques. *L'État-monde: libéralisme, socialisme et communisme à l'échelle globale: refondation du marxisme.* [The World-State: Liberalism, Socialism, and Communism on a Global Scale. Rebuilding Marxism.] Paris: PUF, 2011.

———. *A Political Ecology of Common People.* Translated by David Broder. New York: Routledge, 2024.

———. *Théorie générale: théorie du droit, de l'économie et de la politique.* [General Theory: A Theory of Law, Economics, and Politics.] Paris: PUF, 1999.

Coutrot, Thomas. *Libérer le travail.* [The Liberation of Work.] Paris: Seuil, 2018.

Cukier, Alexis. *Le Travail démocratique.* [Democratizing Work.] Paris: PUF, 2017.

Lahire, Bernard. *Les structures fondamentales des sociétés humaines.* [The Fundamental Structures of Human Societies.] Paris: La Découverte, 2023.

# 1 The One-Party Model

## A Revealing Development of the Party-Form

*The Communist Manifesto* of 1848 did not specify how a "communist party" should be organized. The term "party" should indeed be taken in the older sense of a political current within society. However, such a "party" was supposedly already at work within the working class through the small national organizations that claimed to be part of it. These were called upon to join forces on a global scale under the slogan: "Proletarians of all countries, unite!" Yet, in reality—we can see this more clearly with the benefit of hindsight—these organizations were in themselves a radical novelty, emerging during a moment when a group of militant intellectuals, of whom Marx and Engels were the leading figures, rallied to the cause of the "working class." These theorists endeavored to conceptualize the working class's experience of the class struggle by linking it to the social order of modern society and its "revolutionary" potential against the old society—a potential concentrated first in the bourgeoisie, then in the proletariat. Throughout the second half of the nineteenth century, this alliance under popular hegemony searched for its own political path by gradually organizing itself into a "party" in the modern sense, the general outline of which was defined during the Second International. The various national parties that were born from 1917 onward took extremely different forms, depending on the local contexts and historical situations. An essential divide was established between two institutional models that were nevertheless comparable in certain respects: the one-party model (Chapter 1) and what I call the "party-among-others" model (Chapter 2). What follows is less a historical analysis than it is a reflection on the problems facing the party-form as such. The vicissitudes of these vanished political parties reveal, as if under a magnifying glass, the contradictions inherent in them.

DOI: 10.4324/9781003512356-2

The intellectuals involved here are not simply individual *defectors*. They are representative of the fraction of the "bourgeois class" whose privileges derive essentially, not from *capitalist property*, but from their functions *within* the organization of society in the broadest sense. For this reason, their relations with common people are of a different order. This "party" must be considered in the context of the "triangular duel" that structures the modern form of society. Among the "competent," certain social strata appear to have some reason to associate themselves with members of the working class fighting for a different social order. This encounter was particularly evident in the revolutionary processes of the early twentieth century, which saw the emergence of an unprecedented party-form.

The sequence of events from 1917 onward involved, as we know, a certain number of forks in the road. Within the Russian Empire, the alliance between the popular classes (workers and peasants) and some of the "competent" led to the elimination of both the capitalist part of the bourgeoisie and the older, premodern property-owning classes. Thus, the "competent" gradually found themselves at the helm of a new class order, which then structurally reproduced itself. A similar process took place in China, but without the complete elimination of capital-power. In the "West," the split between two Internationals gave rise to two branches of socialism, one of which, though dazzled by the Soviet experience, nevertheless maintained a radical socialist and internationalist outlook, while the other evolved toward a certain entente with capitalist market logic, eventually tending to subordinate itself to it. In the peripheries of the "Global South," alliances between the "people" and the "competent," whatever their relation to the legacy of Marx, gave rise to or promoted national revolutions against premodern forms of domination and imperialism—at least until neoliberal globalization ended up recuperating its "elites." The spirit of "socialism" has nevertheless survived or reappeared there in various forms. This rough panorama will serve as the basis for the analysis that follows. Before turning in Chapter 2 to the common model of Western anti-capitalist parties, I shall first deal with the one-party model, focusing on two major figures: Lenin and Xi Jinping.

## Lenin: The Unexpected Emergence of the One-Party Model

In the Soviet revolutionary process, Lenin, who was its mastermind, deserves our consideration on several counts. On the one hand, he was at the center of a multifaceted revolutionary ferment, of which Enzo Traverso's book, *Revolution: A Cultural History*, provides an extensive overview.[1] Lenin took the lead of a movement that destroyed the old, premodern Russia and opened a richly promising new horizon. Moreover, he gave Marxism a new world horizon by calling on dominated peoples to revolt against their oppressors. Finally—and this is the point that will hold our attention—he was the initiator of a specific type of party system, the "one-party model," which was decisive for the sequence of events that followed. I will nevertheless be brief on the subject and confine myself to laying down a few milestones to distinguish the Soviet case from the more problematic case of China.

The debate most often focuses on the so-called Leninist conception of a revolutionary political party. But isn't this an illusion? As Marcel van der Linden explains, in the period preceding the seizure of power, Lenin had certainly elaborated a theory of the party that he felt was appropriate for Russia.[2] "Lenin combined the Kautskyian and Narodnikian ('populist') traditions: the German-Marxist idea of introducing revolutionary ideas from outside, and the Russian concept of a conspiratorial elite organization."[3] In reality, no such party ever existed. Prior to October 1917, Van der Linden writes, "the core of the party was still made up of workers."[4] It was not the intelligentsia that played the decisive role, but a group of organized members of the Russian working class, a very undisciplined group at that. As soon as they seized power, Van der Linden continues, their numbers were multiplied by 10 or 20 within a few weeks. From then on, he concludes, the Leninist party project was shattered. What happened? How did the one-party model, an institutional arrangement that neither Marx nor the other founders of socialism had ever envisaged, come into existence? The fact is that Lenin, from 1917 onward, would go on to ban and eliminate the competing parties—Mensheviks, anarchists, and Socialist Revolutionaries. Moreover, at the 10th Congress of the Russian Communist Party in 1921, he prohibited the formation of internal factions from which competing parties could re-emerge. Does this mean that, from the very outset, the creation of a "one-party model" was an integral part of Lenin's idea of a socialist society? I leave it to historians to determine more precisely the trajectory he followed.

Let us confine ourselves to examining the situation that was created and the conditions for its relative sustainability. This is an immense topic that must be studied within the complexity of the world-system. Here, let us focus on the relationship between the one-party model and the overall "socialist" *organization.* Having wiped out the capitalists, the competent remained the sole masters of the game. To use Gramsci's concepts, they *dominated* through a strictly hierarchical process of exclusive organization, which gave them the ability to exert coercion effectively, including through the most extreme forms of violence. Moreover, they *ruled* through their ability to define supposedly common ends, forging, for a time at least, a consensus that stemmed from the experience of manifest revolutionary achievements, such as the emancipation from previous "feudal" servitudes, the improvement of women's legal status, the development of education, etc. Subterranean traces of this initial impetus remained present to the very end. Without them, Gorbachev's utopian *perestroika* would be unintelligible. But, very quickly, it became necessary to relay artificially produced ideals, of which the Stakhanovite movement was a famous example. This did not prevent a growing apprehension, including within the party, of the economic irrationality of a purely organizational order, or the general population's gradual perception of the arbitrariness of state power. The economic machine obviously became an estate that the party held collectively. In other words, a private organization assumed responsibility for public affairs and control over citizens' lives.

This was certainly a regime of domination and exploitation, but it is inaccurate to call it "state capitalism" because it did not follow a strictly capitalist logic. It was not based on *competition between shareholders* in the struggle to maximize their surplus value, the source of their power; rather, it was based on *competition between members of the organization*, institutionally declared "competent," in a struggle to maximize their prestige, the source of their power. This is the sense in which we can speak, sadly but rightly, of "real socialism." Oriented toward the production of concrete use-values, defined through a top-down approach—as highlighted by Agnès Heller's concept of "dictatorship over needs"—it, too, remained a prisoner of "abstract" logic, a logic of hierarchical accumulation of power, which concretely threatened the life and fate of humans and nature.[5] Soviet society experienced the most extreme forms of domination and repression because it found itself alienated from this hierarchical organizational power orchestrated by the competent within the one-party model.

## Xi Jinping: The Exaltation of the Party of the "Competent"

The one-party model, inherited from the USSR, has gradually turned the Communist Party of China into the party of the competent, in the specific sense that I give to this term—those who hold the competent authority to provide management or expertise. Xi Jinping, without using such an expression, has worked in this direction both ideologically and in practice. I will begin by considering the *doctrine* of the current president of the People's Republic of China, insofar as it is supposed to frame his policies. I will then use a socioeconomic approach to decipher what this discourse masks: on the one hand, the relationship between the single party and the state; on the other hand, the relations between the three "primary social forces"—capital/competence/common people—that make up the "triangular duel."

### *A Hermeneutic Reading*

Jérôme Ravenet's work, *Xi Jinping between Marx and Confucius*, offers a deliberately empathetic interpretation of Xi Jinping's thought.[6] Xi Jinping, who, in his youth, gave himself the pseudonym "the joyful philosopher,"[7] has surrounded himself with historians of political thought. Among his close associates, Wang Huning—who became the Communist Party's fourth-ranking member in 2022—has paid particular attention to Jean Bodin's concept of sovereignty, understood as the "absolute and perpetual power of a republic."[8] However, in Ravenet's view, and I think he is right, Spinoza appears to be his true inspiration as he distinguishes between the (political) "power" (*potestas*) of a ruler and the "power" (*potentia*), insofar as it exists, of the entire people, even if it is based on a mixed government that combines democracy and aristocracy. In this diversion of Spinozism, Ravenet notes, Xi Jinping just adds a monarchical dimension. Yet, he never exalts "*potestas*-power."[9] *Collective power* is always what he has in mind, a form of "*potentia*-power" that knows how to "make room for consent and common utility"[10]—or, in other words, one that can adopt and support "the point of view of the masses," to use a common expression. This can be ensured through a variety of procedures, such as popular assemblies at all levels, dialogue with micro-political parties or ethnic representatives, widespread state unionism, and academic discussions. Thus, socialist democracy, which is not "representative" but "*consultative*,"[11] constantly learns from the people, so as to satisfy their demands. This is the "mass line" that the party itself must abide by; otherwise, it will fail, for its legitimacy is essentially moral. The same applies to the president. This is the surprising "Marxism" to which Xi Jinping claims to adhere—one that, as we can see, realizes the promises, not of the Enlightenment, but of classical "absolutism," allegedly taken up by Lenin.

This "Sinicized Marxism," as it is officially called, is just as closely related to Chinese traditions. Among them, the oldest is "Legalism," which appeared at the beginning of the Qin dynasty (221–206 BCE), under the influence of Han Fei. This author, above all others, is indeed "Xi Jinping's favorite, judging by the number of times he is quoted in his speeches."[12] Following in Jacques Gernet's footsteps, Ravenet highlights how Han Fei, a theorist of social totality, insists on "the standardization of the rules of law in criminal, scientific, administrative, and military matters throughout the newly unified territory."[13] This is the root of the meritocratic principle that would later flourish during the Song dynasty (960–1279 CE), well before Western modernity. Xi Jinping has sought to promote this principle specific to Chinese culture during the "New Era," of which he is the herald.

Nevertheless, Confucianism, now thriving throughout the Chinese world, is the main component of this Sinicization. The crucial point in this regard concerns the relationship between the law and morality. While legislation has no business dealing with morality in European modernity, the situation is quite different in China. Xi Jinping writes, "We must insist on the alliance of the law and morality in state governance. The law is morality built into written legal rules, and morality is the law rooted in the human heart. [...] This must ultimately lead to their symbiosis."[14] According to him, morality is "the foundation of the law, while the law guarantees morality."[15] This is the context in which the "socialist rule of law" is defined. Law and morality are merged in such a way that amendments to legislation must be compatible with "the interests of the masses,"[16] the criterion of a moral social order. The task of the party is to uphold this principle and to censor its own actions accordingly. This implies, however, that the party makes "the people its censor of last resort"[17] by remaining attentive to popular expectations. Xi Jinping, whose speeches are always *homilies*, therefore insists more on morality than on the law.

It is in this double context, meritocratic and moralistic, that the role of the party is conceived. Based on the co-optation between members who accept party discipline, the party's vocation is to provide the nation with political leadership—not to run everything, but to monitor everything. Internal debates, supposedly at least, play out in secret. And, on pain of succumbing "to the particular interests of Capital,"[18] the public expression of politics in the press must remain the monopoly of public authorities. This does not mean, however, that the party has exclusive rights to political speech and action. Indeed, as Ravenet adds, "Chinese socialist policy is not discussed in the press, but it is *discussed*."[19] For, unlike party members, ordinary citizens, who enjoy a fairly extensive (but monitored) freedom of association, can express themselves openly and even protest—admittedly within strict limits—to criticize, not the party line, but the conduct of those in charge, at least up to a certain point, as can be seen on social networks. However, the prevalence of morality (which is assessed by a higher authority) over the law disqualifies the very idea of an independent justice system. This opens the door, I might add, to the worst kinds of repression, including the death penalty, of any independent political initiative likely to hinder the party's stranglehold on the social order.

In this endeavor to synthesize "Marxism" and Chinese traditions, I find it interesting to note that Xi Jinping's arguments are based on a certain "class analysis." Three "classes"—although this term is not clearly to be taken in a Marxist sense—are said to be present: the "bourgeoisie," the "middle class," and the "proletarian class." The middle class is also referred to as the "political class"[20] or the "ruling elites."[21] The "proletarian class," in relation to the latter, is generally referred to as "the people" or the "popular masses."[22]

> Chinese society, Xi explains, is destined to become, as largely or broadly as possible, a society of average affluence, i.e., a nation governed in the interests of the middle class (not the bourgeois class, nor the proletarian class, and even less the global superclass), the priority being to strengthen the share of this class within China's demographics and to broaden the popular basis of power.[23]

It remains to be seen, of course, whether this is indeed the right way to view the configuration of class structure in modern-day China.

### *A Realistic and Critical Reading*

If we turn now to the works of sociologists, economists, and political scientists, they most often refer to the Chinese political economy as "state capitalism."[24] This expression implies, on the left, a critical assessment, and on the right, an acknowledgment of the universal vocation of capitalism, coupled with the regret that, in this case, it is the work of a state controlled by a totalitarian party. In contrast to this *doxa*, Rémy Herrera and Zhiming Long[25] point out that, in today's China, land and most banks are publicly owned, and that the public sector plays a fundamental role in the economy, owning 19 out of the 21 largest companies and controlling the downstream supply chain, which determines everything else. Why then, they ask, should we label this economy as capitalist rather than socialist? In a monumental PhD dissertation,[26] Nathan Sperber carefully analyzes the weight of the single party in the public and private sectors, and within the later, the formal and informal confrontations between capitalists and state representatives at the micro, meso, and macro levels. Although he uses the term "state capitalism," he rejects the monistic liberal interpretation. "In sociological terms, private capital-owners and party-state cadres are best seen as two distinct class actors."[27] In his view as well, the public sector, predominant in areas that have an impact on all sectors, "occupies the 'commanding heights' of the Chinese economy… . From this, it should follow that the public elite is the dominant collective actor and that the private capitalist class comes second on the scale of social power."[28] He adds, however, that in the long term, the private sector could gain the upper hand, due to its faster rate of accumulation.[29]

N. Sperber's investigation seems very convincing to me. I only question the relevance of the concepts that punctuate his analysis. He depicts two social actors that he refers to as "class actors": a "private elite" and a "public elite." The owners of capital, representatives of the "capitalist class," clash with the cadres, "representatives of the state," who are in fact the cadres of the Communist Party, which controls the state apparatus at all levels. "The party commands, the state obeys," according to an adage that comes from Mao, as N. Sperber reminds us elsewhere.[30] This may be true, but is it enough to allow him to speak of a "party-state?" According to my Marx-inspired metastructural approach, the foundations of which I will develop in Chapter 4, a modern state politically articulates class relations, "nation relations," and gender relations on a national territory. The state apparatus is the set of functional institutions that a modern state, as a nation-state, oversees (parliament, government, army, police, administration, finance, etc.). That control of it is at stake in the political struggle between classes—a struggle that, as we have seen, takes the form of a "triangular duel," with the dominant class having two poles: capital and "competence." It is therefore inaccurate to claim that the state is the exclusive representative of a certain class or that it "faces" another class.

The Chinese Communist Party, like the Soviet one before it, was born of an alliance between common people (both city dwellers and peasants) and a fraction of the competent. In the USSR, the competent, having eliminated the capitalists, found themselves in a position of exclusive control of the state apparatus. In China, the capitalist sector, which could be mobilized against imperialist domination, was spared by Mao, then brought to the fore by Deng Xiaoping. The competent, organized as a single party, have given themselves the means to dominate the state apparatus, by doubling it with a party apparatus that controls it at all levels, having also placed the armed forces under its express control. Thus, the single party does not represent the state; it represents the structural prevalence of "competence" within the state, in the sense I have given to this term as a dominant social force distinct from capital.

But the state apparatus is not the whole of what we might call "state apparatuses." It is rooted in what Gramsci identified as the instruments of the state, meaning the set of public and private institutions that make up "civil society" and are constitutive of the state as a political relationship between classes. The single party certainly exercises close and continuous control over this "civil society." However, this society, not only in its private dimension, but also in its public dimension, has its own dynamics. This is the reason why the power of the single party is by no means secure in the long term.

In short, the situation of China cannot be said to be that of "state capitalism," for other social forces tend to prevail. Historically, the pre-eminence of competence-power can be derived from its ability to take the lead in the great modern Chinese revolution that swept away the old social structures and thereby restored (in its former imperial dimension) Chinese national identity against the imperialisms to which it had fallen prey—a double claim to fame. But how did competence-power manage to maintain this privileged position? It was certainly able to draw on the dictatorial procedures at work in the revolutionary process that had discredited the existing rule of law without yet establishing a new one, in this "dangerous interregnum where monsters are born," to quote Gramsci. Today, its grip may be reinforced by a Xi Jinping-style discourse that mobilizes traditional cultural resources: meritocratic exaltation, which is devoted to hierarchical power; and the subordination of law to morality, a religion for those who have none that comes to sacralize those at the top of the hierarchy. But isn't it necessary to explain both the resilience of the dictatorial machine and the ideological production that tends to elicit assent to the balance of power? And can this be done in any other way than by relating them to the structural mechanisms that determine them? In this case, we must turn to Bourdieu and his analysis of the reproduction of "competence" as a distinct form of class power that is based on the possession, not of (capitalist) property in the market, but of competent authority within organizations and society. The mechanisms at work in China are indeed the same as those observed in any modern society. Higher education, in the broadest sense, is one of its essential elements. In the absence of parents with college degrees, it has become difficult to gain access to higher education in good conditions. Beyond this example, we must understand that the pole of competence as a whole is endowed with a structural capacity to reproduce itself.

However, we cannot leave it at that. For, during the revolutionary process, this structural component of the pole of competence "in-itself" awakened to become a self-conscious "for-itself" through the invention of the single party, which came to *instrumentalize* the exercise and reproduction of competence-power. In reality, however, this process encountered a substantial contradiction. For, the more the party became reserved for the competent themselves, and the more its popular components (peasants, workers, and employees) became a minority, the less the party maintained what had constituted its social power: its foundational claim to be the site of an *alliance* between common people and the competent. It lost a defining feature of competence-power, which is that it is exercised, unlike capital-power, through a discursive relationship by which the competent seek the assent of those below them by appealing to their reason. The party was thus increasingly perceived to be the agent of a higher class. And, just as in the Soviet case, this agent was given a *hierarchical* form that was specific to its "competent" pole and that was radicalized as it became the primary force of domination. Power was then concentrated in such a way as to silence all opposition and authorize the worst forms of violence. This is not the place to describe these phenomena, which are now amply documented. I merely suggest that this is what we can call a "socialist dictatorship," if, as I propose, "socialism" is understood to be the proper horizon of competence-power, as opposed to "communism," as the perspective of common people.

Throughout this history, as "social relations" were transformed, so too were the "productive forces" and the means of communication between individuals and in the world at large. It is hardly surprising that people have been able to make themselves heard, notably through social movements—which, since Tiananmen, however, have remained more or less scattered and short-lived. Their limitation, today, as is the case with all the revolts that have shaken the world in recent decades, is that they do not open any defined perspective. "Socialism," as an alternative to "capitalism," provided an almost universal point of reference. This marker has disappeared. And we are reduced to questioning the course of social revolts and the signs they might give of the quest for a future.

According to my Marx-inspired metastructural approach, the (capitalist) market and the (socialist) plan are nothing other than "mediations" of "immediate" relations, i.e., cooperative-discursive relations. When common people, within large corporations or in street protests, come to demand, beyond limited concrete reforms, not better socialism or more capitalism, but the freedom to express what they, as citizens, think is best for everyone, something is bound to happen. And this "something," in today's China, has also been manifesting itself, analogously, over a longer period, on another stage: through the attitude of a fraction of the competent, who refuse to let themselves be drawn into the false pretenses of "Sinicized Marxism," as seen in large circles of intellectual opinion, and even within the Communist Party.

This is expressed in many ways. It is not a question of head-on opposition, but of putting forward other theoretical and political approaches. This is quite clearly the case in the "Centers for the Study of Marxism Abroad" that exist in many departments of philosophy, where numerous researchers devote their dissertations to the Frankfurt School, analytical Marxism, or the French tradition. The same goes for the Schools of Marxism, present in all universities, to which foreign lecturers, presumedly Marxist or not, from various disciplines are invited. Chinese traditions are certainly studied there too, and rightly so; but students also prepare dissertations on Husserl, Bataille, Sartre, Althusser, and Agamben, among others. None of these prepares the teachers and students to appreciate, or even to tolerate, the Sinicized Marxism of Xi Jinping.[31] The famous writer Fang Fang, for example, throughout the duration of the confinement in Wuhan, kept a daily blog—written in an extremely polemical style, and sometimes read by 10 million Internet users—in which she strongly attacks the "nationalists" and what she refers to as the neo-Maoist "far left," while ardently calling for the free expression of everyone.[32] As a result, she is now rigorously censored. But, even severely repressed, Chinese literature and films bear witness to the fact that the cultural landscape of China, a land of successive revolutions where tenacious memories take root, cannot be reduced to the shiny grayness of "Xi Jinping thought." Given the radical absence of democracy that prevails in China, as well as the central role China plays in imperialism, one can imagine the worst. And with each day passing, new causes for concern emerge. Yet, nothing prevents us from thinking that Chinese society, with its wealth of heroic and tragic experiences still alive in its collective memory, may be opening up to new horizons.

For the purposes of this book, what must we learn from the history of the two great one-party models of the past century for our analysis of the contradictions of the "party-form" today? Despite appearances, if I have ventured to delve into these cases, it is because they both demonstrate how, in different historical conditions, the popular struggle against capital-power implies an alliance-struggle with and against competence-power, by virtue of a constraint inscribed in the triangular duel constitutive of the modern form of society—a constraint that common people have regularly seen turn against them. If this is so, we can expect to find the same types of constraints and contradictions in the trajectories of the "Marxist parties" specific to the West, the memory of which still permeates left-wing culture today.

## Notes

1 Enzo Traverso, *Revolution: An Intellectual History* (London: Verso, 2021).
2 Marcel Van der Linden, Jean-Numa Ducange, and Jacques Bidet, "Labor history, tournant de « l'histoire globale » et marxismes," [Labor History, the "Global History Turn," and Marxisms.] *Actuel Marx* 62, no. 2 (2017).
3 Van der Linden, Ducange, and Bidet, "Labor History," 189.
4 Van der Linden, Ducange, and Bidet, "Labor History," 190.
5 The case of Cuba, where a one-party model appeared and developed in incomparable historical conditions, will not be discussed here.
6 Jérôme Ravenet, *Xi Jinping entre Marx et Confucius: décryptage philosophique d'un socialisme chinois* [Xi Jinping between Marx and

Confucius: A Philosophical Decryption of Chinese Socialism], 2 vols. (Paris: Volubilys, 2022).
7 Ravenet, *Xi Jinping*, 2: 78.
8 Ravenet, *Xi Jinping*, 1: 123.
9 Ravenet, *Xi Jinping*, 1: 66.
10 Ravenet, *Xi Jinping*, 1: 178.
11 Ravenet, *Xi Jinping*, *passim*.
12 Ravenet, *Xi Jinping*, 1: 353.
13 Ravenet, *Xi Jinping*, 2: 35.
14 Quoted in Ravenet, *Xi Jinping*, 1: 226.
15 Ravenet, *Xi Jinping*, 2: 29.
16 Ravenet, *Xi Jinping*, 1: 202 et passim.
17 Ravenet, *Xi Jinping*, 2: 24.
18 Ravenet, *Xi Jinping*, 2: 105.
19 Ravenet, *Xi Jinping*, 2: 102.
20 Ravenet, *Xi Jinping*, 2: 105.
21 Ravenet, *Xi Jinping*, 1: 367 et passim.
22 Ravenet, *Xi Jinping*, 2: 350 et passim.
23 Ravenet, *Xi Jinping*, 1: 203.
24 See, for example, Marie-Claire Bergère, *Chine: le nouveau capitalisme d'État* [China: The New State Capitalism] (Paris: Fayard, 2013).
25 Rémy Herrera and Zhiming Long, *La Chine est-elle capitaliste?* [Is China Capitalist?] (Paris: Éditions Critiques, 2019).
26 Nathan Sperber, "Rethinking State Capitalism: The Chinese Political Economy in Comparative Perspective" (PhD dissertation, L'École des hautes études en sciences sociales, 2017).
27 Sperber, "Rethinking State Capitalism," 329.
28 Sperber, "Rethinking State Capitalism," 330.
29 Sperber, "Rethinking State Capitalism," 330.
30 Nathan Sperber, "L'État du Parti," [The State of the Party.] *Le Grand Continent* (June 20, 2019); See also Nathan Sperber, "Les rapports entre parti et État en Chine aujourd'hui: une clé de lecture soviétique," [The Relations between the Party and the State in China Today: A Soviet Reading.] 73, no. 1 (2023).
31 It turns out, for example, that Althusser's book, *On the Reproduction of Capitalism*, translated into Chinese a decade ago, is now receiving an enthusiastic reception in student, philosophical, and literary circles, giving rise to hundreds of written contributions circulating on the web—and that takes a certain audacity. With its focus on "ideological state apparatuses," it clearly appears to open a pathway to a critical alternative to "Sinicized Marxism." On the CNKI (China National Knowledge Infrastructure), the largest digital portal for university publications, researchers can find details on the hundreds of dissertations and diplomas published in Chinese concerning Althusser. Clearly, the party can no longer monitor everything.

This can also be seen at the International Marx Conference, held every two years under the aegis of the School of Marxism at the venerable Peking University, attended by many leaders of the various schools of Marxism, and where all heterodoxies are on display.

32 See Fang Fang, *Wuhan Diary: Dispatches from a Quarantined City*, trans. Michael Berry (New York: HarperVia, 2022).

## References

Bergère, Marie-Claire. *Chine: le nouveau capitalisme d'État.* [China: The New State Capitalism]. Paris: Fayard, 2013.

Fang, Fang. *Wuhan Diary: Dispatches from a Quarantined City.* Translated by Michael Berry. New York: HarperVia, 2022.

Herrera, Rémy, and Zhiming Long. *La Chine est-elle capitaliste?* [Is China Capitalist?]. Paris: Éditions Critiques, 2019.

Ravenet, Jérôme. *Xi Jinping entre Marx et Confucius: décryptage philosophique d'un socialisme chinois.* [Xi Jinping between Marx and Confucius: A Philosophical Decryption of Chinese Socialism]. 2 vols. Paris: Volubilys, 2022.

Sperber, Nathan. "L'État du Parti." *Le Grand Continent* (June 20, 2019).

———. "Les rapports entre parti et État en Chine aujourd'hui: une clé de lecture soviétique." 73, no. 1 (2023): 21–39.

———. "Rethinking State Capitalism: The Chinese Political Economy in Comparative Perspective." PhD dissertation, L'École des hautes études en sciences sociales, 2017.

Traverso, Enzo. *Revolution: An Intellectual History.* London: Verso, 2021.

Van der Linden, Marcel, Jean-Numa Ducange, and Jacques Bidet. "Labor history, tournant de « l'histoire globale » et marxismes." *Actuel Marx* 62, no. 2 (2017): 181–96.

# 2 The Mixed Legacy of the Bygone Class Party

I call the "Western" form of communist parties, which appeared where the hegemony of capital prevailed in the triangular duel, the "party-among-others" model. Armed with the conviction that they represent the future of humanity, these parties call on their militants to be exclusively committed to this cause. In their efforts at self-reflection, they are not interested in parties in general, but rather in the party-form specific to them, as parties opposed to the hegemony of capital. Each one of them is "*the* party"—both that of the "working class" it must lead to victory, and that of "the nation" it is called upon to lead. These two elements are found in all communist parties, although to a variable extent from one country to another depending on social and historical circumstances. I have chosen to take as an example the contrast between the party of the nation, as Gramsci conceived it, and the party of the working class, a common model that Althusser criticized. Both Gramsci and Althusser certainly perceived the "crucial problem": the duality of the dominant class. They approached it in different ways, one more positively, the other more negatively. Let us examine what these two leading thinkers can teach us and what their analyses stumble upon regarding the requirements of popular political practice.

## Gramsci: In Search of a Popular-National Will

It seems enlightening to approach Gramsci from the point of view of Althusser's criticisms of him and the responses that must be given.

In a manuscript entitled *What Is to Be Done?*[1] written in 1978 and published in French in 2018, Althusser reminds us that Gramsci, in his approach to modern society, focuses not on the brutality of a

DOI: 10.4324/9781003512356-3

"mode of production," but on the hegemony exercised within it by a "historical bloc." "Hegemony," as he understands it, defines political power insofar as it imposes itself effectively and sustainably, not through pure violence, but as a force enveloped in consensus. Thus, it is only as a *politically* ruling class that an *economically* dominant class asserts its power. This is performed through the intermediary of certain intellectuals—in both the broad and narrow sense—who serve as agents of consensus, their activity taking place within institutions such as "the Churches, the school system, the political parties, the trade unions, and so on."[2] For this reason, even if these intellectuals are private citizens, they must be considered "state apparatuses" of capitalist power. Althusser, as we have seen, takes up this concept and develops it into a theory of ideological state apparatuses, thus following in Gramsci's footsteps. However, he levels two criticisms at Gramsci that need to be examined.

First, Gramsci focuses solely on the superstructure, whereas it is only from the infrastructure that both the constitutive violence of the capitalist class division and the socioeconomic composition of the process of capital accumulation can be grasped. Althusser claims that Gramsci remains limited by his own set of concepts, which are purely political, while the socioeconomic level represents for him no more than a backdrop. Having thus configured politics within the contours of the "superstructure," "[w]e would look in vain for vestiges of the classes and the class struggle."[3] The violence of economic relations is subsumed under *acquiescence*, by which political relations are established. Hegemony emerges when the use of force dissolves into consensus. Althusser writes, "we here witness a veritable operation of substitution… . We start out from the distinction force/hegemony and, by the end, force has disappeared."[4] It seems to me that, in reality, Gramsci approaches the question quite differently. His intention is to attack capital-power. But he approaches class domination from the angle of competence-power. These are not his terms, but it is certainly his idea. For him, in fact, the party must see itself as a collective intellectual, capable of building its own cultural hegemony. And this is the condition for the people to be able to prevail in the economic and political arena.

Althusser's second criticism goes further. By locking himself into a conceptual matrix limited to politics, Gramsci allegedly ends up transforming "historical materialism"—a form of *realism* that articulates the economic and the political—into a pure philosophy of history. "Marxism," as it derives from Marx, is certainly to be understood as both a "materialist philosophy" and a "materialist theory of history." But these are two distinct things, not to be confused. However, when Gramsci refers to Marxism as "the philosophy of praxis," this is not a code name intended to hide his Marx-inspired thinking from his jailers when he was a political prisoner. "The term philosophy of praxis unquestionably expresses Gramsci's own thinking."[5] "Gramsci is the first theorist to have taken a real interest in the phenomena of the superstructure, the state, and the ideologies."[6] But he questions the meaning of events rather than their causes and effects. This means that, where one would expect economic-political explanations, we are only given cultural-political interpretations, based on pure descriptions. "*Gramsci is not a theorist of history, but a reader of history*."[7] History, interpreted this way, delivers its own meaning, which lies in its manifest orientation toward emancipation. All it needs now is the strategic discourse that will guide our practices to hasten its natural progress.[8]

Recent Gramscian studies tend to demonstrate Gramsci's historical realism and the heuristic potential of his concepts.[9] This is the direction in which I would like to take up the question again. Gramsci, in fact, considers the role of the party from a completely different, more realist perspective, one centered on a "nation-based Marxism" that is indeed a theory, not a philosophy of history. And it is paradoxically Althusser who, in his *Machiavel and Us*,[10] offers a properly *Gramscian* reading of *The Prince* in which he underlines this essential point: the ruler's objective, as a modern ruler, is to make Italy, like France and Spain, a *nation*. It is to build not just a state, but a nation-state, a *national space*. Machiavelli is not just a precursor of absolutism; he also saw absolute power from a popular point of view. To eliminate the territorial power of feudal lords, a ruler, according to him, must rely on the common people suffering from feudal oppression and longing for peace, tranquility, and freedom. He therefore seeks to establish legality in this sense, an unfailing "power of the law" that inspires fear and commands respect through the fiction of its loyalty to supposedly transcendent religious authorities.

Such a state can only exist within a defined territory, morally unified by language and customs, and militarily defended by indigenous popular forces. Machiavelli therefore provides an early analysis of the class struggle and its political horizon. But, as we see, his motivation is national. And this is indeed how Gramsci, before Althusser, understood Machiavelli's approach: "a democratic intervention in Italian history and politics," as Vittorio Morfino puts it, "where 'democratic' means the construction of a unitary state and an absolute monarchy that, with the force and consent of the popular masses, destroyed the feudal elements of Italian society at the time."[11] Similarly, a "modern ruler," organized as a political party, must work toward the "formation of a popular-national collective will."[12] The imperative of "economic reform," he adds, is very present. But the proper object of his analysis is the national gathering of social and cultural forces against a power identified as capitalist. In this, as Dominico Losurdo points out, Gramsci, as an heir to Lenin, departs from the tendency of "Western Marxism" to develop outside the concept of "nation." "Absent from the Frankfurt School, the national question also plays no relevant role either in Lukács or Bloch's writings."[13] Nor in the French tradition of communism, we can add. Although the "nation" is present in the practice of French communism,[14] it is virtually absent from theoretical reflection. French Marxism is first and foremost a *class-oriented Marxism*, the key concept of which is exploitation, while "nation-oriented Marxism" revolves around the concept of domination. These two concepts are not mutually exclusive, but it is necessary to identify the relationship between them.[15]

## Althusser: In Search of the Dictatorship of the Proletariat

Althusser, an avowed disciple of Gramsci despite the criticisms he leveled at him, tackled these issues nearly half a century later, in a completely different historical context. At the end of the 1970s, a decade during which the *Programme commun* united the entire French left, he came to a radical critique of his own party (although his aim was clearly more general). He developed his ideas with great force in several writings intended for a general audience at the time.[16]

One of these is *Les Vaches noires* [Black Cows], written in 1976 and published posthumously in 2016.[17] This text was written in reaction to the party line adopted at the 22nd Congress of the French Communist Party in February 1976. In it, Althusser agrees with the party's decision to distance itself from the USSR as symbolized by the abandonment of all references to the "dictatorship of the proletariat." Yet, if he still uses this expression, it is with regard to the *concept* it originally designated. Precisely in the name of *communism*, it is against the idea that the ultimate objective is *socialism*, understood as a "mode of production," a "stable society" that places the major means of production under the control of a regulatory and protective state.[18] Of course, "to nationalize is to destroy the bourgeois class in its strongholds."[19] But, beyond this "first phase," everything remains to be done, and this "beyond" is already here. The other battle to be waged concerns "mass democracy," which is to be promoted in all spheres of society (the workplace, schools, neighborhoods, etc.).[20] The "dictatorship of the proletariat" is the exercise of power by the exploited class insofar as it "destroys the state apparatus."[21] It must revolutionize all aspects of social, material, cultural, and political life—in affinity, so he believed, with the "Cultural Revolution" in full swing at the time. The prospect of a political struggle within all public and private institutions is, of course, common to all communist parties. But the strength of Althusser's "cry" lies in the fact that it manifests, in the form of lofty doubt and premonitory despair, how infinitely more formidable the challenges of "communism" and the transition to it from "socialism" are, compared to those of mere "socialism"—which, at the time, may have seemed to be looming on the horizon.

The second text to be analyzed had a very different editorial destiny. It was first published in April 1978 in the newspaper *Le Monde*, under the title "*Ce qui ne peut plus durer dans le Parti communiste*" [What Can No Longer Be Sustained within the Communist Party], and then it was immediately published in book form by Maspero.[22] Althusser wrote this piece on the occasion of a "historic" meeting of the Central Committee, held on April 26–27, 1978 as the Communist Party faced poor results in the legislative elections, after spearheading the *Programme commun* only to see the Socialist Party prevail over it. The text appeared in *Le Monde* from May 24 to 27.[23] Althusser covers both the party's *practice* and *theory*. "What can no longer be sustained," according to him, is its vertical, top-down way of operating, with no real upward movement. This, he writes, is the party's "military dimension." Freedom of discussion certainly exists in the local cells, but it stops there. Everything is decided by the Political Bureau and leaders at the federal level, who are secretly co-opted. As for theory, the Communist Party has transformed it into "evolutionary positivism." The state, in its "monopolistic" phase, allegedly becomes a "unique mechanism," directly at the disposable of popular power. As such, there is no more question of "destroying" it. Supposedly, we are already in the "antechamber of socialism." In reality, Althusser writes, the only way out is to "leave the fortress." Of course, it is necessary to "establish alliances." But the proletariat can only count on itself and the strength of its organization. The party, according to him, must therefore return to the revolutionary line that had prevailed in 1934–1936, that of the "popular committees"—in other words, "unity at the grassroots" and "unity in struggles," as future slogans would proclaim. Clearly, here was something to shake up the party-form.

I think it is worth noting that this political position was the counterpart of a vast theoretical project aimed at clarifying and putting Marxism back on its feet. Althusser is representative of a generation of intellectuals who, faced with the fiasco of the "Communist" International, tried to put an end to a certain Marxism that had transformed into a mix between a philosophy of emancipation and a philosophy of progress, a simple and powerful discourse, but one that could be manipulated for various uses. His most important contribution is, it seems to me, a rehabilitation of "historical materialism,"[24] understood to be distinct from a "philosophy of history" in that it is precisely not a *philosophy*, but solely and properly a *theory*. A theory among others, to be judged according to the same criteria: its coherence as a conceptual system and its capacity to account for empirical realities. What distinguishes "historical materialism" from other theories, whether sociological or economic, is its ambition to be *general*, i.e., to integrate these various dimensions into a *general theory* of societies and their history. As soon as it takes as its object "our era," the one in which we live (which still must be defined), it integrates the critical dimension of a discourse to which *citizens* can refer when aiming to be "responsible" actors, i.e., capable of answering for their choices, in line with citizens' demands as historical subjects. At the very least, anyone wishing to engage in the tasks this requires must push the conceptual analyses and empirical investigations—the two sides of "theorization"—as far as possible in this direction.

Althusser did not just make this epistemic clarification. He also made his own unique contribution to the revival of historical materialism. Contrary to a certain economism prevalent at the time, he sought to establish a junction between the *structural* and the *discursive*—in other words, between the order of social structures and the order of social discourses. To this end, he proposed two original concepts that, to my mind, form a coherent pair: "interpellation" and "ideological state apparatuses."[25] By this he meant that capitalist power, in his words, functions not only through repression, but also through ideology. If these "state apparatuses" are described as "ideological," it is in the sense that, through their organs, "they speak" ("*ça parle,*" to use Lacan's concept). Their discourse must be deciphered in its materiality, in the economic-legal fabric of the institutions constituting the social order; and this is where we must fight it. It is present across the entire spectrum of educational, cultural, religious, associative, trade union, and police institutions, among others. And, to Althusser, this discourse finds its unity in the fact that it uniformly calls for submission to the reigning order. We only emerge as subjects when we are already "interpellated." Althusser sought to decipher such a mechanism of domination insofar as it is exercised not just on the basis of capitalist property (in the discourse of the "boss"), but also on the basis of the entire organizational fabric of society. He thus had in mind a class power that permeates all social institutions and is likely to impose its domination beyond the supposed abolition of capitalist property. It was against this power that, under the guise of the "dictatorship of the proletariat," he called for a "class struggle" aimed at radical democratization.

In my view, however, Althusser lacked the concepts required to move forward with this. He therefore failed to decipher not only the nature of the relationship between the structural and the discursive, but also the nature of the *other form* of "class power." Nor did he decipher the foundations of the necessary struggle-alliance with it. There is therefore no such thing as "Althusserian politics." If this is so, it is not because of his supposed "structuralism," but, as we shall see, because he is a prisoner of what I call "common Marxism," which, for lack of a correct understanding of the modern class structure, is incapable of identifying the contradictions of the party-form. This is also true of other left-wing organizations with anti-capitalist pretensions.

In short, Althusser and Gramsci put us on the path to a popular practice of politics. What remains is to try to bring the enterprise to its conclusion. This requires an adequate theoretical construction of the class relationship conceived as a "struggle-alliance" within the "triangular duel" constitutive of the modern social order, under the aegis of a common discursive potential: the "nation" of the nation-state. Only then will it be possible to push the theoretical demonstration beyond the world-system to the ecological concept of the world-nation as popular practice.

## Notes

1 Louis Althusser, *What Is to Be Done?* [Que faire?], ed. G. M. Goshgarian (Cambridge, UK: Polity Press, 2020).
2 Althusser, *What Is to Be Done?*, 50.
3 Althusser, *What Is to Be Done?*, 37.
4 Althusser, *What Is to Be Done?*, 55.
5 Althusser, *What Is to Be Done?*, 46.
6 Althusser, *What Is to Be Done?*, 30.
7 Althusser, *What Is to Be Done?*, 43 (emphasis in original).
8 "…the philosophical thinking that subtends it: *normative* and, consequently, idealist thinking." Althusser, *What Is to Be Done?*, 37. Gramsci transformed Marxism into "*absolute humanism*," i.e., a finalist conception of history, "*absolute historicism*." Althusser, *What Is to Be Done?*, 41 (emphasis in original).
9 See Yohann Douet, *L'histoire et la question de la modernité chez Antonio Gramsci* [Antonio Gramsci's Conception of History and Modernity] (Paris: Classiques Garnier, 2022). The author takes stock of all recent studies, essentially Italian ones, and convincingly develops the theme of Gramsci's "realist historicism."
10 Louis Althusser, *Machiavelli and Us*, trans. Gregory Elliott, 2nd ed., ed. François Matheron (London: Verso, 2011).
11 Vittorio Morfino, "Image et fonction de Machiavel chez Gramsci," [The Image and Function of Machiavelli according to Gramsci.] *La Pensée* 406, no. 2 (2021): 124.
12 Morfino, "Image et fonction de Machiavel," 128.
13 Domenico Losurdo, *Antonio Gramsci dal liberalismo al "comunismo critico"* [Antonio Gramsci: From Liberalism to "Critical Communism"] (Rome: Gamberetti, 1997), 205.
14 The French Communist Party's role in the "resistance" during World War II marks, as we know, a great moment, just like its resolute commitment against "French Algeria."
15 The "meta-Marxist" approach that I present in *A Political Ecology of the Common People* (New York: Routledge, 2024) is inspired by Gramsci in various respects. On the one hand, it takes his approach to the concept of state apparatuses from an angle that reveals the *state-based* nature of private institutions, which I also apply to firms. On the other hand, it adopts his approach to class domination in terms of a "hegemonic bloc," which I develop through the problem of the "regime of hegemony." In my view, however, the most important Gramscian concept, the one in which all others are reflected, is his conception of the "nation." The role of the party, as a "modern ruler," according to Gramsci, is to make the nation what it should be: free from class domination. And it is this concept that I propose

to redeploy in various ways by bringing it to its political-ecological conclusion: the world-nation.

16 If Althusser was a member of the French Communist Party, it was obviously because he held this institution and its historical role in very high esteem. This is not the place to discuss this opinion of his, but only to examine the way in which he understood the crisis that the party went through at the turn of the 1980s.

17 Louis Althusser, *Les vaches noires. Interview imaginaire* [Black Cows. An Imaginary Interview], ed. G. M. Ghoshgarian (Paris: PUF, 2016).

18 Althusser, *Les vaches noires*, 247.

19 Althusser, *Les vaches noires*, 238.

20 Althusser, *Les vaches noires*, 242–43.

21 Althusser, *Les vaches noires*, 227.

22 Louis Althusser, *Ce qui ne peut plus durer dans le Parti communiste* [What Can No Longer Be Sustained within the Communist Party] (Paris: Maspero, 1978).

23 The quotes that follow are from the text published by Maspero in 1978.

24 See Marx's sixth thesis on Feuerbach: "Feuerbach resolves the religious essence into the human essence. But the human essence is no abstraction inherent in each single individual. In its reality, it is the ensemble of the social relations." It must be emphasized that this is not a historical-theoretical assertion, but an anthropological-philosophical one. This thesis invites us to study "social relations" and "social practice." However, because this is not its aim, it provides no conceptual framework for a theory of society. It says nothing about what these social relations are. It only rules out the opposite philosophical choice, that of *methodological individualism*. These are two opposing epistemologies based on two opposing anthropologies.

25 See my radical critique of this approach in Jacques Bidet, "Le sujet interpellé: au-delà d'Althusser et de Butler," [The Interpellated Subject: Beyond Althusser and Butler.] *Actuel Marx* 61, no. 1 (2017). I present an alternative theory of interpellation by defining it through the concept of metastructure.

## References

Althusser, Louis. *Ce qui ne peut plus durer dans le Parti communiste.* [What Can No Longer Be Sustained within the Communist Party.] Paris: Maspero, 1978.

———. *Les vaches noires. Interview imaginaire.* [Black Cows. An Imaginary Interview.] Edited by G. M. Ghosgarian. Paris: PUF, 2016.

———. *Machiavelli and Us.* Translated by Gregory Elliott. 2nd ed. Edited by François Matheron. London: Verso, 2011.

———. *What Is to Be Done?* [Que faire?] Edited by G. M. Goshgarian. Cambridge, UK: Polity Press, 2020.

Bidet, Jacques. "Le sujet interpellé: au-delà d'Althusser et de Butler." *Actuel Marx* 61, no. 1 (2017): 184–201.

Douet, Yohann. *L'histoire et la question de la modernité chez Antonio Gramsci.* [Antonio Gramsci's Conception of History and Modernity.] Paris: Classiques Garnier, 2022.

Losurdo, Domenico. *Antonio Gramsci dal liberalismo al "comunismo critico."* [Antonio Gramsci: From Liberalism to "Critical Communism."] Rome: Gamberetti, 1997.

Morfino, Vittorio. "Image et fonction de Machiavel chez Gramsci." *La Pensée* 406, no. 2 (2021): 120–29.

# 3 The Fatal Contradictions of the Movement-Form

If populism is a political form that directly unites the populace with a leader, without going through the deliberative and elective bodies that characterize the party-form, then the "movement-form" is particularly well suited to it.[1] Other ways to embody it exist as well. Indeed, there are versions of populism across the entire political spectrum: from the far right to the "far" left, including the traditional right and the so-called center.[2] Today's left-wing populism in southern Europe seems to be linked to a political situation specific to this region: the exhaustion of the anti-capitalist party-form, combined with the persistence of a revolutionary tradition whose underlying habitus are maintained through a web of unions, associations of all kinds, and cultural means of revolt. The distinctive feature of this populism is that it takes on a "movement-form" that explicitly presents itself as an alternative to the "party-form," which can no longer take charge of, unite, and orchestrate this disparate potential. The movement-form competes with the party-form on both the social and environmental fronts. This is the perspective from which I will analyze, as carefully as possible, the works of the two authors who are jointly engaged in the theoretical legitimization of left-wing populism, Ernesto Laclau and Chantal Mouffe.

I will leave aside their joint work, *Hegemony and Socialist Strategy* (1985).[3] Their aim in this book is to conceptualize a "new left" beyond social democracy. They intend to "radicalize democracy," i.e., to extend its scope by drawing on the demands for equality that, especially since 1968, have gone beyond the economic sphere to include feminism, anti-racism, and urban and anti-institutional struggles. In this sense, they accuse social democracy of clinging to the "working

DOI: 10.4324/9781003512356-4

class," defined by its central place in the production process and supposedly in charge of forging an alternative to the form of social domination whose essence is perceived to be capitalist. To Laclau and Mouffe, the capital/labor relationship is just one among others of equal importance, within a complex and fluctuating society where identities are constructed at the crossroads of multiple social relationships. New social movements, of which Laclau and Mouffe are the heralds, are becoming the new motor for change. The left must therefore be rebuilt on a broader basis. Let us grant them that it is indeed appropriate to consider social relations other than class relations. Yet, their *modus operandi* is radical: sweeping aside all materialist types of realism (of which Marxism has no monopoly), they stick to a strictly "political science" approach to politics. This is the sense in which they use the Gramsci-inspired concept of "hegemony." They invoke prestigious philosophical authorities, such as Saussure, Wittgenstein, and Derrida, from whom they retain the idea that society is structured like a language.

During a later period, post-2000, which will be the focus of my analysis, we see the emergence, through works now carried out separately, of a new concern: the degeneration of social-democratic parties into center-left parties, alternating with center-right parties to carry out indistinguishable policies. Faced with the spread of neoliberalism, the current situation, as they see it, is dominated by the rise of populism, in which they intend to take part. This project overlaps with the previous one but does not do away with it, since it focuses on left-wing populism. But the central issue for them has become the (re)construction of "a people." Laclau draws his arguments from semiotics and psychoanalysis; and Mouffe, from the academic context of political philosophy. The new emancipatory dynamic that they have in mind, however, is still based on social movements, which they call upon to build a populist hegemony on the left by "equating" the various "democratic" (i.e., egalitarian) demands these movements put forward. The reconstruction of the left has metamorphosed into the construction of "a people." Without disavowing themselves, the theorists of the new left have become the theorists of left-wing populism.

Laclau and Mouffe's theory sets out to challenge a "Them" that rules from above, conceived as an "oligarchy," which presumably brings together the summits of both capital and technocratic power. This overturns the vision of a certain left that had conceived this couple under the unilateral and composite scheme of "capitalism."

However, this remains purely descriptive, devoid of conceptual unity. It is at the grass roots that the perspective becomes unified, through the discursive chain of "demands" merging under the aegis of a leader, a true *deus ex machina* who is destined to emerge and whose word is golden. As we shall see, this intervention, which ends up neutralizing the theoretical and critical potential of modern culture, is likely to come into contradiction with the expectations of the very population it is aimed at.

## Ernesto Laclau: Populist Politics as Rhetoric

Laclau's work recaptures, in secularized form, the prophetic breath of the "liberation theology" that flourished in Latin America during his youth. The difference is that those committed theologians had drawn on a Marxist analysis of social classes and the state that was particularly sensitive to the center/periphery arrangement of the world-system. For Laclau, the order of discourse tends to be given as the measure of reality. This is particularly evident in his other major work, *On Populist Reason*, written 20 years after *Hegemony and Socialist Strategy*. Its starting point is something like a general, more or less universal social structure: "a dichotomic division between unfulfilled social demands, on the one hand, and an unresponsive power, on the other."[4]

This "chain" of heterogeneous demands emanates, of course, from a "plurality of subject positions."[5] The task of making them converge is now assigned to "rhetoric." "Rhetorical mechanisms" are what "constitute the anatomy of the social world."[6] "Discourse is the primary terrain of the constitution of objectivity as such."[7] The "deepest" objectivity, without a doubt. It seems to me that Laclau treats the categories of the social sciences in the same way that Saussure treated those of ordinary language. They only define differences and relationships between differences, without ever making the thing itself appear—in this case, the living totality of a community, which can only be given in a political discourse that expresses how much it is both lacking and expected. "There is a fullness of the community that is missing."[8] The "people" spoken of here is not a pre-existing fact. It is missing because it is not yet. It can only exist when united by populism, whose work is to be understood as a "performative operation constituting the chain as such,"[9] a speech act. "[T]he construction of the 'people' will be the attempt to give a name to that absent fullness."[10] There is certainly a profound truth in all of this. The community must be built; what is missing is its very being. But there is an idealistic bias at play here between the people and "the people." "The people," as fullness, is certainly "what is missing." Nevertheless, let's not forget the reality of the people, in the common sense of the term, as a particular human community occupying a territory as its own, and structurally voicing an irrefragable "this is ours," guaranteed by the fury of arms. This is a formidable "objectivity," defining an *exclusive* "we" that a populist rhetorical ontology only assumes by sublimating it.

In this rhetorical logic, Laclau affirms that "the equivalence between unsatisfied democratic demands"—their mutual recognition as equivalent even though they are heterogeneous—must be given a common signifier, emptied of any particular demand and capable of signifying all the others, as in the case of a synecdoche where the part is substituted for the whole. This "empty signifier" must *express* the fullness of "the people we are missing." "[T]here is emptiness because that void points to the absent fullness of the community. Emptiness and fullness are, in fact, synonymous."[11] It is significant that Laclau uses the "market" in post-1989 Eastern Europe as an example of an "empty signifier."[12] In itself, the "market" is an economic signifier, but it transmits its value to every link in the chain, symbolizing the community that is found but still "missing." Other examples he uses include "workers" and "levelling instinct."[13] Laclau certainly gives us some fine lessons in political rhetoric, on familiar territory commonly referred to as the "battle of words"—a cultural battle within the political struggle, a political battle within culture. A place of affects as much as of understanding. For my part, I will venture the hypothesis that, in this populist discourse, be it right-wing or left-wing, it is quite simply the word "people" that plays this role; and that it only plays it so well because of its semantic richness (of denotations and connotations) and the ambiguities attached to it: popular people, civic people, ethnic people, people-nation, people-community, chosen people, rebellious people, insubmissive people, admirable people, eternal people.[14]

The thesis that makes "populist reason" a form of "rhetorical reason" leads to another one, which is the last word of Laclau's visionary discourse. To his mind, only a charismatic leader can give the "empty signifier" the fullness of its meaning. A master of rhetoric will find the right words and the significant "name" of the entire chain. From this singular name proceeds "the 'people' (the equivalential chain [*sic*].)"[15]

"But," he adds, "the extreme form of singularity is an individuality"—that of a leader. "In this way, almost imperceptibly, the equivalential logic leads to singularity, and singularity to identification of the unity of the group with the name of the leader."[16] The leader's words set the people in motion. It is hardly surprising if some great leaders have recognized themselves in Ernesto Laclau's discourse.

## Chantal Mouffe: Converging Demands for Equality

At first glance, nothing seems to predispose Chantal Mouffe to this populist adventure, on a conceptual level at least. Her own work is essentially located in the workshop of philosophical debates between democrats and liberals of various schools. However, if I propose to dwell on her work at greater length, in the form of a near monograph, it is partly because of the reception it has received from populist-movementist leaders, and partly because it enlightens us better than any other on the ins and outs of the movement-form (*versus* the party-form), notably the links it establishes between the primacy of discourse and the pre-eminence of leaders.

### *Social-Democratic Memories*

Before getting into the theoretical heart of the matter, it seems enlightening to start by evoking the social and political imaginaries Chantal Mouffe uses in her latest book, *For a Left Populism*.[17] This does not mean that we should judge her *theory* according to her political *opinions* or *feelings*. Nothing could be more theoretically disastrous—all the more so as the *other* imaginary, the other collective memory, its competitor on the left, which I shall *nostalgically* evoke in the style of Enzo Traverso, is now just as obsolete. Let us just consider the three-act *narrative* that underpins her *analysis*.

*Act 1.* The period from the 1930s to the 1970s was the era of "social democracy," which asserted its hegemony against capitalism. It was an age of "Keynesian compromise," of the "social-democratic Keynesian welfare state," when the "social-democratic model" prevailed.[18] In the (social-democratic) memory of Chantal Mouffe, the "working class" of communists, Trotskyists, anarchists, Labour activists, revolutionary trade unionists, operaists, self-managing workers, and a variety of other discordant "leftists," with an active network of social and cultural forces during this half-century, simply did not exist... Perhaps it disappeared without a trace? This is a question for another day. But in Mouffe's account, all the conquests of this era are attributed to an anonymous "social democracy," a true Providence for us all.[19]

*Act 2*. After 1970, neoliberalism ushered in an age of "consensus in the center." Certainly, the emergence of new social movements heralded a new course.[20] But social democracy gave in to neoliberalism. It succumbed to the "consensus" model, where the remaining choice was between a "center-left" and a "center-right" that pursued roughly the same policies. The sign of the awakening could only come from forces outside this left-right composite, where the only clashes were between partners in collusion. Indeed, various forms of "democratic resistance" emerged not only on the left, but also on the far right:

> At the beginning, most of the political resistances against the post-democratic consensus came from the right. In the 1990s, right-wing populist parties like the FPÖ in Austria and the Front National in France began to *present themselves* as aiming to give back to 'the people' the voice of which they had been deprived by the elites.[21]

On the other hand, nothing to note on the left: the neoliberal model, coupled with "possessive individualism," "did not face any significant challenge until the financial crisis of 2008."[22] The social-political struggles that punctuated this era do not enter the author's conception.[23] All in all, we lived through "years of relative apathy," waiting for the moment when a "political awakening" would come.[24]

*Act 3*. The 2008 crisis marked the beginning of the "populist moment." The system, now in crisis, was called into question by "anti-establishment movements, both from the right and from the left."[25] It thus became possible to break down the "consensus," to establish a new "frontier" that revives antagonism, "a frontier between the 'people' and the 'political establishment.'"[26] Chantal Mouffe sees this illustrated in the movements that emerged during the years that followed, associated with Syriza, Podemos, La France Insoumise, occupations of squares (Indignados, Occupy Wall Street, Nuit Debout, etc.), and the dynamics of social movements. She emphasizes that neoliberalism has struck more *broadly* than previous forms of capitalism. And, from a populist perspective, this fact should be taken positively. Every cloud has a silver lining: "this provides an *opportunity* [for the left], since the number of people affected by the neoliberal policies is much higher than those who are usually considered traditional left voters."[27] Thus, this populist moment was also, let us say, a moment to seize. People's misfortunes are, in a way, probably due to the fact that history is a bit cynical, and this is an asset for a "progressive alternative."[28] But this is only on the condition that the "social question" is broadened to include "diverse forms of subordination around issues concerning exploitation, domination or discrimination."[29] The author concludes that it is important that left-wing populism prevails over right-wing populism. "In the next few years," this will be "the central axis of the political conflict."[30] In short, in her view, our salvation can only come from a certain populism, from a victory of the left within populism…

I will not blame the "political theorist"[31] for focusing on the "moment," i.e., on the conjuncture. Timing *action* that is appropriate for the moment is precisely the temporality of "politics." But how can we understand this *moment* if not by linking the conjunctural approach to, on the one hand, an analysis of long-term, political-economic *social structures*, as well as their contradictions and immanent trends and counter-trends; and on the other hand, to their interferences with the variable configurations of the world-system, from which the chaos of conjunctures and the course of periodization are periodically renewed? Are we merely "beings of the moment?"

### *Restoring a Normal, Functional Order*

At the heart of this book, we find an original conceptual framework that Chantal Mouffe had begun to develop, after *Hegemony and Social Strategy*, in a series of texts intended for different audiences with different expectations, making them interesting to relate to one another.[32] The theme of returning to a certain *normalcy* emerges from the outset. To form a people by rebuilding the left, which has become perverted by joining the center, it is necessary to *reestablish* a *normal* order by drawing a clear "frontier" between the right, where various forms of domination coalesce, and the left, where the forces for emancipation come together. Therefore, for Mouffe as well as Laclau, there is an essential divide. Let's call it the "Great Antagonism." This is what separates "Power," which is attributed to the "caste" or "oligarchy" (those at the top of the financial sector and the state apparatus), from the "People." And the confrontation between them takes place on a political stage that must be "restored"—a recurring and essential term, which betrays Mouffe's discreet functionalism—by developing a hegemonic project on the left that unites all "social groups" prey to domination by equating all demands for equality.

From here on, things get complicated because this great divide between the dominant and the dominated, vaguely analogous to the one we might find in the writings of the disciples of Marx or Bourdieu (and many others), intersects with a second one that stems from internal debates in contemporary political philosophy. Chantal Mouffe draws inspiration, among other, from the "liberal-democratic" theory of C. B. McPherson. In the pair indicated by this dual adjective, she sees the *contingent* confluence of two traditions: *liberalism*, centered on freedoms, private property, and human rights; and *democracy*, focused on equality and popular sovereignty. An enlightened philosophy would obviously not push us to pit these two demands—freedom and equality—against each other, but rather to seek to unite them. Nevertheless, this divide, formulated in terms of two traditions, bears a (vague) resemblance to the left-right confrontation. And Chantal Mouffe, knowledgeable of the drift of social democracy, would not want to be drawn into soft, centrist positions.

She manages to get out of this difficulty through an unexpected detour. She turns to a sulphureous political theorist, Carl Schmitt, who subverts this peaceful philosophical-political space by arguing that "the political" is, in essence, conflictual. If conflict disappears, politics is no longer needed. The central pairing is therefore not freedom/equality, but friend/enemy. This seems to have been a real baptism by fire for Chantal Mouffe, who must now face "the enemy." She pulls it off elegantly, and without much effort, by arguing that she certainly takes up this idea, but in the context of our "modern Western societies," where liberal democracy prevails. It is therefore not a question of *enemies* to be eliminated, but of *adversaries* to be fought while "respecting" them. It is not about "destroying" the adversaries; it is about combating their "ideas," for the confrontation must not "lead to civil war."[33] Quite the insight, indeed. But this is a far cry from Carl Schmitt and his theory of the "partisan," who also carries a gun. This is the conceptual reversal that Chantal Mouffe describes as the transformation of antagonism into "agonism." We are called to a *respectful* fight.

What is this "fight" all about? It takes place peacefully in various spheres of society, taking on the full range of popular forms of resistance and initiatives. It goes without saying that the "strategy" proposed by left-wing populism is expected to lead to electoral victory. But in this context, the opponents must be respected, i.e., given the opportunity to express themselves and organize politically. Political conflict can therefore only be conceived within the framework of "pluralism," now a key concept for Chantal Mouffe. What democrat would dare to contradict her?

### *Approaching the Great Antagonism through Pluralism: The Magic of the Palimpsest*

Yet, after this remarkable conceptual advance, how shall we conceive the great clash between Power and the People, the motivator of populism? It seems that the question has simply disappeared. "Pluralism," as a constitutive element of "liberal democracy"—the pluralism of political parties—is the functional device[34] by which all social, ethnic, cultural, and other conflicts must be resolved. At least this is what is expected of it. This means that the same procedures, the term of which is *parliamentary*, must be used to deal with the "Great Antagonism" and "Miscellaneous Antagonisms," as I will call them. The former opposes Power to the People, while the latter concern the multiple contradictions that can be found within a society.

From this general agonistic alignment arises a true miracle. The Great Antagonism dissolves purely and simply into diversity. Of course, the power of those above, the "caste," is still present. But Chantal Mouffe, as a "political" theorist, has nothing else to say about it; for "the theory of politics," thus developed in the pure register of *politics*, has no appropriate concept for the analysis of societies. It can do no more than transpose *class, "race," and gender struggles*—a set understood to include exploitation—*in a political confrontation between peacefully opposed projects*, at least in "our democracies." On this political stage, where we are called upon to "fight," the Power of the ruling classes, adorned in a toga, moves forward as a "Project"—a project-in-action, of course, but one whose implementation can be analyzed as a *political process* in which all those who share it take part, i.e., right-wing supporters at all levels. The people's Adversary, the Power of the "caste," has been transformed into an adversary called "the right," which includes all those who support it. The conflict between "Us and Them" is calmed by becoming an affair "between us," right-wing supporters against left-wing supporters. In any case, for Chantal Mouffe, this is the *normalcy* that must be re-established by "restoring the frontier" between "Us and Them."

If the disappearance of the Great Antagonism in the magician's hat goes unnoticed, it is because Mouffe uses an ingenious stratagem. It consists of superimposing various layers of theoretical formulations, more or less fused together, like a *palimpsest*, in such a way that after reading and re-reading, it is often difficult to understand what all the fuss is about. Her driving thesis, proudly stated, a real *bravado* against liberals, is that politics exists only through *conflict*. But does she mean conflict between groups in general? Between the People and Power? Between the right and the left? Within a community? Between liberal values and democratic values, which are inevitably in tension? Between freedom and equality? Her readers often have every reason to hesitate because these various pairs are mentioned in the same terms, i.e., in terms of "tension," "confrontation," "conflictuality," "coexistence," "conciliation," between opposing elements. In reality, her readers mustn't worry; it's all of these things together. An "equivalential chain," as it were. Incidentally, this is what makes the book so "philosophically" appealing, and at the same time accessible, due to the *vagueness* of the subject matter (which corresponds to the "vagueness" that Laclau makes the hallmark of politics)—at least as long as one doesn't try to figure out how this scholarly political writing really works. For that's when the puzzle begins.

Where Laclau resolves political problems through *rhetoric*, arguing that social categories themselves are rhetorical, Mouffe resolves them through *politics*, arguing that everything is political, the social order being made up of opposing "projects." Indeed, who could deny that the right and the left traditionally present themselves as two great opposing projects, which are broken down into a variety of micro-projects concerning all the points of friction affecting the various social categories? It would seem, however, that "politics," conceived in this way, gets locked within its own discourse. It is quite true that social contradictions can ultimately only be resolved through political means. However, this in no way means that they can only be conceived through the lens of politics. As a political theorist, Chantal Mouffe has no other concepts to analyze reality than those of political philosophy. It is on the basis of "demands for equality" (which Laclau also makes his "starting point") that her democratic empathy leads her to discover inequalities likely to turn into "subordination"—a common denominator concept that subsumes them all by emptying them of their own proper scope ("exploitation," reduced to subordination, ceases to be the principle of capital accumulation). Her investigation is limited to the examination of these "democratic demands," and her objective, to the search for their convergence. Discourse analysis takes the place of sociopolitical analysis—to which it seems we must object that, although social relations certainly give rise to practices that, being endowed with meaning, are indissociably material and "discursive," it does not follow that they can be dissolved in this discursivity. It is certainly necessary to ensure that these discourses, which are differently overdetermined, come together in common projects. But this is only made possible by examining the social relations themselves. For can we imagine proposing a political theory that makes no reference to a theory of society?

What is Chantal Mouffe's position on this point?

### *"The Social Order" as Pure Contingency*

The main components of her position are developed in *The Democratic Paradox* and *On the Political*. I will concentrate on her latest work, *For a Left Populism*, and more specifically on its "Theoretical Appendix," which reproduces the book's "canonical" formulations, as it were. There we find, outlined in broad strokes, two complementary poles: the "social order" and the "social agent." Let's start with the first one.

Mouffe and Laclau emphasize that their aim is not to produce a doctrine, but a "strategy." They deal specifically with "political practice." However, they can only propose a practice with reference to a certain theory. In this sense, they speak of a social "ontology," a concept with a scholarly pedigree. But they also use more common terms, to be taken in a broad sense, such as "paradigm" and "philosophy," which express their thinking just as adequately. The word "ontology," however, best demonstrates their lofty ambition: to open a new page in the history of theories of "social being." Several themes are closely associated with it: the idea that society is structured like a language; the idea that language shapes society; the idea that this performative language is political in nature; the idea that language is action, and that political action is discursive action. But these various statements must be read in light of the first: society is structured like a language.[35] This is precisely how Chantal Mouffe understands it. "The people" itself is to be understood as a fact of language. The people, of course, exist as an empirical fact, but this is foreign to the political ontology considered here.

> A left populist strategy," Mouffe writes, "is informed by an anti-essentialist approach according to which the 'people' is not an empirical referent but a discursive political construction. It does not exist previously to its performative articulation and cannot be apprehended through sociological categories.[36]

Obviously, this theme does not assert itself in the wilderness, but on the stage of a theoretical-political theater where it opposes others. No need to be a rocket scientist to understand that the aim here is to get rid of "historical materialism."[37]

In reality, the structural order, at least as defined by the Marxist tradition (as Gramsci and Althusser remind us, each in their own way), is itself "ontologically" discursive. But Mouffe's theory takes us to a completely different, *discursive* conception of "ontology."[38] "Every social order is the temporary and precarious articulation of hegemonic practices whose aim is to establish order in a context of contingency."[39] The social order is made up of " 'sedimented' practices" that "conceal the originary act of their contingent political institution."[40] Everything, then, is contingent—not just social *practices*, but also the *situations* in which they introduce the constitutive order of a society. This order, it is true, allows us to go beyond pure contingency, since an "ordered" relationship will exist between the elements that it articulates... But there is no "deeper objectivity that would be exterior to the practices that brought it into being." There is no "ultimate rational ground."[41]

Let's question this last proposition. Let us imagine that a capitalist, established in an old textile-producing region, discovers that his businesses are still profitable but that he could make more profits elsewhere. He closes them down and ships the material a thousand kilometers further east, where labor is cheaper. What sense does it make to say there is "no ultimate rational basis" for the social order in which such an event takes place, nor for such a practice to be carried out? What kind of "rational basis" are we talking about here? And why should it be "ultimate?" In reality, what we have here is indeed a form of *rationality*—a real and binding "social logic" specific to the competitive capitalist order, which requires each competitor, on pain of extinction, to maximize profit, whatever the social or environmental consequences. This rationality is not "ultimate." One might think it could be abolished. But from this idea, Chantal Mouffe, by virtue of her own ontology, believes she can deduce that everything "social" is nothing but the deployment of hegemonic *practices*, which are "always the expression of a particular configuration of power relations."[42] She leaves aside the question of what social mechanisms *produce* such an accumulation of power, making such projects and practices conceivable and possible. She looks away from this *unintentional* "social order" that sociologists, economists, anthropologists, historians, legal scholars, etc., seek to decipher, and within which intentional acts take place. In her approach, there is simply capitalist power, a power allegedly "established" by capitalists, acting through "originary acts." "Every existing order is therefore susceptible to being challenged by counter-hegemonic practices."[43] In short, we are among human actors: what some have done, others can undo. Once again, quite the insight.

In a "materialist" approach, things are taken quite differently. It is true that social structures do not exist outside of the practices that reconstitute them at every moment. These are the ABCs of any theory of reproduction, Marxist or otherwise. But these practices are themselves unintelligible outside of the structures that give them their own logic. Practices are inseparable from the language in which they are given, while structures are silent. The conceptual work necessary to approach reality consists precisely in seeking to understand how these two terms, the structural and the discursive, are linked. For Chantal Mouffe, however, "social order" is born of political practices, groundlessly, in a way. The ground is there, evoked, invoked, presupposed. For there *is* neoliberalism, of course. But it is not part of the subject matter, which is strictly political. Class relations, just like gender or "race" relations, only appear in the form of the "social demands" to which they give rise. Under these conditions, they are very likely to have only a minimal "ontological" value.[44]

### *"The Social Agent" as a Bouquet of Identities*

We obviously cannot understand the social order without considering correlatively the social subject. Thus, Chantal Mouffe moves from "the social order" to "the social agent," i.e., the "subject."[45] In her view, the identity of social agents refers not a social structure, nor to their place in such a structure, but to the "subject positions" they hold and the "intersections" between them. "The social agent is constituted by an ensemble of 'discursive positions' that can never be totally fixed in a closed system of differences."[46] The identity of the subject is the product of "specific forms of identification."[47] As a political philosopher, Chantal Mouffe does not seem concerned by the social complexity that gives rise to this plurality of discourses interfering in the singularity of an individual subject. According to her, it is the "discursive positions" that define "the identity of the subject." The reflection she offers us does not belong to *social theory*, but to *political theory* in its purest form, a specific discipline which scrutinizes subjects by observing their speeches. Discourse analysis replaces the analysis of social realities. The concrete social agent, in fact, "is constructed by a diversity of discourses, among which there is no necessary relation but a constant movement of overdetermination and displacement."[48] She adds that this is what "makes possible the generation of totalizing effects."[49] In other words, it is not social relations that are overdetermined and inter-determined between themselves, but discourses.

If then we are to understand the conditions and practices of young African women who perform undeclared work looking after the children of wealthy families in privileged neighborhoods, what must be considered according to Chantal Mouffe is not a set of *social relations*, such as those based on class, sex, age, or nationality (class-race-sex interference and inter-determination), but these women's self-consciousness—namely, their supposed *discourses*. This is allegedly the site where identities are subject to interferences and overdetermination, where the "totalizing effect" between various demands is possible. Of course, this is only true, she adds, in a "field characterized by open and determinate frontiers."[50] This statement is obscure. Let's try to make it clearer. One might think that this "field," where discourses "are determined" and "totalized," is constituted by a "set of social relationships" (being young, being a woman, coming from the colonies, being a domestic worker) that are quite different from the relations of language to which they give rise. The latter can only be understood from the former. Moving from a *social situation* defined by class, race, and gender to a social *consciousness* certainly presupposes that people collectively "speak out" to give meaning to their social struggles. Semantics and rhetoric constitute the pivot of "politics." But—and I will further develop this point later using my metastructural theory of "interpellation"—the discursive is not external to the structural; it is inherent to it. As such, it cannot take its place. And yet, the analytical framework Mouffe offers us here is that of the "political field," in its orchestral singularity—a pure field of discursive positions where polyphonic subjects assert themselves.

What Chantal Mouffe ultimately lacks, as we can see, is the very concept of "social relations," in the sense of relations that individuals maintain between each other based on their positions within "structural" relations (in the broad sense of the term), i.e., class, gender, and "nation" relations. A *social relation* cannot be reduced to the *discourse* to which it gives rise, which is only one element of this "structural relation." The identification of these young African women as activists in a victorious struggle, one that succeeded in modifying social relations somewhat, will certainly change something in their identities and existence, both enriched thanks to new solidarities. Their lives will be transfigured for some time, and perhaps marked forever. But the "deeper objectivities"—class, gender, nation ("race")—which are the locus of the problems to be resolved, will remain powerfully at work. We can only consider transforming them by taking them in the "objective" unity that they form with each other. This is what remains outside Chantal Mouffe's theoretical framework.

The various gender relations, class relations, or "nation relations" involved in this pluralism of identities are constantly at odds with each other. The invention of the contraceptive pill marked the history of gender relations, not that of class relations. It altered the "intersections" and "overdeterminations" between gender and class. Women, in control of their sexuality, may obtain a better relationship with employment, from which a more combative identity can emerge. Thus, the *discourses* of identity must themselves be related to the variations in the intersections between the *social relations* of class and gender in which they are involved. But discourses do not provide the "ontology" of these relations. In her political discourse, Chantal Mouffe methodologically reduces social relations to discursive relations—methodological idealism. Of course, the goal of emancipation implies that these heterogeneous discourses meet in common projects. But, precisely, this is only made possible by examining the social relations themselves, the heterogeneity of which is reflected in the heterogeneity of discourses, identities, "demands," etc. Otherwise, each of these discourses—"classist," "feminist," etc.—runs the risk of becoming self-complacent.

"The 'identity' of such a multiple and contradictory subject," writes Chantal Mouffe, "is … always contingent, precarious, temporarily fixed at the intersection of those discourses and dependent on specific forms of identification" that are prey to an "essential non-fixity."[51] Certainly. But there is every reason to think that this precariousness, this very discontinuity of identities can be linked to a structural dynamic, to technological mutations and the crises inherent to them, to changes in the balance of power between nations and territories, etc.—in short, to a revolution in social relations. When a mining industry executive or a rural farmer finds himself in the precarious situation of "self-employment," many things change "in their heads." Mouffe would no doubt agree. In her view, however, it is not in the "objectivity" of the social world that we must look for the conditions of convergence between the heterogeneous demands inherent in these various identities; rather, it is in an appropriate language, in a "vocabulary" that orients them "towards more egalitarian objectives," which they can then articulate and communicate on.[52] Hence the praise given to seduction: "A project of radicalization of democracy could therefore appeal to constituencies which so far have not identified with the left."[53] Just as "an ambitious and well-designed ecological project could offer an attractive vision of a future democratic society that might entice some sectors currently within the neoliberal hegemonic bloc."[54] For her, as for Laclau, political theory culminates in communication theory, and politics, in rhetoric.

### *The Mobilization of Affects, the Leader, and the Nation*

However, as we know, it is the "social relations" themselves that need to be transformed. And this supposes that we analyze the structures that make them up, their historical trends, the power relations that emerge at any given moment. Yet, Chantal Mouffe, a political philosopher, has nothing of the sort on her agenda. Indeed, for her, the "social order" is only made up of antagonistic projects, which develop in a context that is nothing more than the sedimented result of the implementation of previous projects. There is no "deeper objectivity."[55] This is what we might call a bold "philosophical decision." However, we must ask ourselves how capitalists are *able* to accumulate so much *power* to nurture such *projects*, and by what processes such a concentration of economic and political power can be constituted. The same goes for the "oligarchy" of the state apparatus. The same also goes for the structures of patriarchy, the configuration of the world-system, and the interweaving of all these social forms. The available "theories" are undoubtedly deficient; but political theorists should be, first and foremost, engaged in the work to overhaul and reconstruct them. To analyze "projects," shouldn't we be seeking to understand the social forces behind them, as well as the factors that bring them into being and weld them together? Chantal Mouffe deals with politics based on politics. At no point does she question the structural conditions of these phenomena; she refers to lived experience, and more specifically to affects.[56]

We can indeed agree that "political identities" are to be understood as a "crystallization of affects" that "provide the motor for political action."[57] We can also "recognize the role of this libidinal energy and the fact that it is malleable and can be oriented in multiple directions, producing different affect."[58] To illustrate this idea, the author uses (at her discretion) Spinoza, Freud, Rorty, and other leading thinkers. She concludes that "the radicalization of democracy requires mobilizing affective energy through inscription in discursive practices that beget identification with a democratic egalitarian vision."[59] Once again, quite the insight. As we can see, her starting point involves a general anthropological statement, essential to the program of any political theory: Affects are something other than interests or inclinations. And she proposes a "progressive" political mobilization, to use her preferred term. However, if we are to judge this operation, we need to take an interest in the "deeper objectivities" that these affects manifest, unless they hide them. It is not enough to *understand* affects; we must seek to *explain* them. Otherwise, we run the risk of understanding nothing at all.[60]

Having taken the "affective turn," Chantal Mouffe takes the liberty of warning us about the "extreme left," who "see their role as making [people] realize the 'truth' about their situation. Instead of designating the adversaries in ways that people can identify, they use abstract categories like 'capitalism,' thereby failing to mobilize the affective dimension necessary to motivate people to act politically."[61] Ah, the noble people! Left-wing populism thus intends to create "a different regime of desires and affects" that starts from "the problems that people encounter in their daily lives" to "reach their affects."[62] It sets itself the task of reformatting their affects in the Spinozist sense of joy—by "offering them a vision of the future that gives them hope, instead of remaining in the register of denunciation."[63] In short, the people are not ripe for critical analysis. Let's talk to them instead about a brighter tomorrow.

It will come as no surprise that, in these conditions, Chantal Mouffe also needs a charismatic leader. "To turn heterogeneous demands into a collective will," she affirms in *Podemos: In the Name of the People*, "it is necessary to have a figure that can represent that unity, and I don't think there can be a populist moment without leadership."[64] She adds that, although "charismatic leadership" can also have "negative effects," this "shouldn't blind us to its importance. It all depends on the type of relation that is established between the leader and the people."[65] She writes elsewhere that "the leader can be conceived as a *primus inter pares*."[66] A reassuring vision, indeed… Yet, isn't it the task of the people themselves, within different groups, to "build equivalences?" Isn't it up to climate activists to discover that they are not climate activists at all if their demands do not also include "social" issues, feminism, anti-racism, etc., just as it is up to feminists, trade unionists, etc., to do the same in their own niches? Unless we'd rather rely on the "affective bonds" that unite the people "with a charismatic leader…"[67]

One point, however, remains obscure in this project to reform affects: the place of nations. Chantal Mouffe rightly points out that "nations" are central to politics for two reasons. On the one hand, they are "one of the crucial spaces for the exercise of democracy and popular sovereignty."[68] On the other hand, "strong libidinal investment [is] at work in national … forms of identification."[69] It is therefore important not to abandon this terrain to the proponents of neoliberal globalization or right-wing populism. It follows that we must offer a positive "outlet for those affects, mobilizing them around a patriotic identification with the best and more egalitarian aspects of the national tradition."[70] What democrat would dare to take the opposite side? On this basis, however, it remains to be seen what this privileged relationship is between affects and nations. Could this marvelous coincidence not also be a dangerous liaison? The secret site of the most prodigious form of repression that weighs on "the political?" This intimate affects/nation relation reveals—but this does not seem to strike Chantal Mouffe—that the hot spot of affects is not located in the adversarial people/oligarchy relation within the nation, but in the compatriot/foreigner relation between nations, which is always likely to veer into an antagonistic friend/enemy relation. Above all, it is necessary to understand the modalities of interference between these two disparate popular "relations," one to the oligarchy, the other to foreigners. Indeed, "politics" brings the adversary and the enemy, the national friend and the foreign enemy, into a loop—not to mention the supposed foreigners from within. Quite the shadow play. It is not enough to declare that the "democratic and liberal" doctrine presented replaces "the enemy with the adversary," as the refrain goes. To be sure, we need to consider another kind of "deeper objectivity," one that is at one with the identities to which it gives rise but does not dissolve in them.

To connect affects to ideas, it is necessary in this case to confront the obscure materiality of the "motherland," which its occupants defend with arms and by various other means. *We love this land because it is "ours."* "This land is our land"—or so it is *declared*, at least, by all nation-states. Critical thinking must therefore take into consideration not only the appropriation and control of the means of production and exchange by a class, or an "oligarchy," but also the exclusive appropriation of a territory by a self-defined community. This is the *other* primary configuration of the modern social order, not that of the class structure, but that of the world-system, which is very much just as real, and which gives rise to another form of opposition between "Us and Them." And it too can be discovered only for what it is through the austere detour of the concept. Chantal Mouffe, for her part, simply makes the nation-state the ground on which a community proposes to build a radical democracy. Yet, this bears a striking resemblance to the social democracy that Chantal Mouffe had condemned to the ash heap of history.

### *The Return to the Social-Democratic Fold*

Whatever the contribution of great leadership, the guiding thread of Chantal Mouffe's thought is indeed her philosophical-political framework marked by the desire to associate the values of freedom, embodied in liberalism, and equality, embodied in democracy.[71] When she writes that a "social order" is structured by "power relations" established through "conflicting hegemonic projects" that confront each other in the "public sphere," she is on the same ground as Habermas: that of "communicative" political relations.[72] What defines communicative action is that it cannot advance (supposed) "truths" without at the same time referring to (alleged) "values" to which it commits itself. On a *philosophical* level, it seems to me that Habermas is right, and this is also how Chantal Mouffe understands it. There is no "democracy," she writes, without "allegiance to the ethico-political values that constitute its principles of legitimacy, and to the institutions in which these are inscribed."[73] But it is the *political* translation of this philosophical proposition that I think is erroneous.

I have explained this at length elsewhere.[74] This appears when Chantal Mouffe, in a formulation that is typical of Habermas, calls for the "antagonistic dimension" of "conflicting hegemonic projects" to be "enacted by means of a confrontation, whose procedures are accepted by the adversaries."[75]

Chantal Mouffe certainly touches on an essential point here. But, to clarify it, we need an analysis (a theory) of the relations between the discursive and structural dimensions of society, which here are reduced to the interplay of "antagonistic projects," presented as the ultimate social reality. What must be explained is how *modern* society, which is classist, patriarchal, and permeated with inequalities and constraints on liberty, specifically produces a public discourse of freedom and equality, which expresses a common sentiment, a "fixed popular opinion," as Marx says on this subject,[76] from which no candidate to leadership can deviate without some risk. The "symbolic imaginary" that Laclau and Mouffe speak of, conceptually disconnected from the structure of modern society, with its contradictions and dynamics, floats in the air, so to speak. As such, neither its emancipatory potential nor the obstacles it encounters are discernible. Yet, this presupposition of freedom and equality is a regular *product* of the social process. To put it in a more philosophical language, this presupposition is "posited," produced. The *theoretical* question is *how* it is produced. Neither the speculative approach to politics nor the rhetorical approach can account for this *production* process. A proper *theory* of society must link the structural and the discursive.

Ultimately, what in my view is required is a *critical theory* that gives the same weight to both these terms, "critical" and "theory." A *theory* that focuses on the materiality of power relations, their conditions and what is at stake. A *critique* that focuses on relations of meaning. Not from a transcendental distance from *what is*, but at the very heart of what is. For, what-is, as a relation-of-power, only *exists* as such in its relation to what-is-said. This is how a potential for self-criticism emerges. Otherwise, in my view, we can neither understand nor explain the class struggle, the gender struggle, and more generally the course of history, in the modern era.[77]

It is true that this is not Chantal Mouffe's ambition. What paradoxically remains outside of her line of inquiry is the fundamentally *political* nature of the "deeper objectivity" that she does not want to hear about, namely the *structures* in which the confrontation between modern hegemonic "projects" is rooted. In other words, more precisely, the *political* content of the "infrastructure" itself. Her approach as a "political scientist" is not *too* political; it is not political *enough*. Or to use her own metaphor, not "deeply" enough. It depoliticizes economics. It thus "deeply" depoliticizes politics itself.

In *On the Political*, she invites us to foster "the agonistic character of politics through the revitalization of the left/right distinction."[78] "What is at stake in the left/right opposition," however, in her view, "is not a particular content ... but the recognition of social division and the legitimization of conflict," even if this divide "certainly refers to opposing attitudes with respect to social redistribution."[79] Let's face it, it's hard to find a more "centrist social-democratic" confession. This opposition, she adds, "brings to the fore the existence in a democratic society of a plurality of interests and demands which, although they conflict and can never be finally reconciled, should nevertheless be considered as legitimate."[80] She makes reference not only to Norberto Bobbio, but also—because everything is possible in this "palimpsest" literary genre—to Niklas Luhmann, for whom "modern democracy calls for ... a clear divide between the government and the opposition..., giving the possibility to citizens to decide between different ways of organizing society."[81] Luhmann, as we know, is a thinker of functionalism rather than antagonism. But Chantal Mouffe also wants society to "function" well, despite the "allegiance" of the various partners to values "in tension" with each other—a recurring set of terminology. Ultimately, *pluralism*, based on a plurality of irreconcilable *interests* and *values*, but between which peaceful coexistence must be ensured, is the central concept of this "left-wing" populism. Capitalism, which Marx said had its natural place in "the icy water of egotistical calculation," has moved, as we can see, into the lukewarm water of pluralism.

Conflict is the essence of politics—appeased conflict. Democracy, understood as the fulfillment of pluralism, has become its own end. The only real enemies, in this world of partner-adversaries who share the benefits of plurality, are those who reject pluralism. The danger, signaled in the very last sentence of *For a Left Populism*, is not that projects imposed from above will prevail over projects developed at the grass roots. It is that "this democratic confrontation will be replaced by a confrontation between nonnegotiable moral values or essentialist forms of identification."[82] Islamic danger? (Right-wing) populist danger? Or (left-wing) extremist danger? It's up to the reader to tick the right box.

In any case, in *The Democratic Paradox*, Chantal Mouffe will have warned us. For what is "paradoxical" is that liberalism and democracy, in their "popular suffrage" dimension, are under "the tension deriving from the workings of their different logics."[83] Conclusion: "pluralist democratic politics consists in pragmatic, precarious and necessarily unstable forms of negotiating its constitutive paradox."[84] In this book, intended for an academic audience, and which makes no mention of the Great Antagonism, Chantal Mouffe, rejecting the theme of *deliberation*, of Habermas's "deliberative democracy," replaces it with the idea of "pragmatic negotiations between political forces,"[85] the subject of which, as we can see, is the "paradoxical" relationship between freedom and equality. The palimpsest superimposes the pairing of political forces and that of values, by means of an obscure "pragmatism" that visibly designates nothing other than the "arrangement" between values and interests (between the "social forces" that bear them). As we can see, Chantal Mouffe's ruses move us far away from Ernesto Laclau's visions.

We can thus understand why the word "socialism," which in 1985 appeared in the title of *Hegemony and Socialist Strategy*, is virtually absent from Chantal Mouffe's later works. In *For a Left Populism*, it seems to me the term only appears once, among the "names" that could be given to mean "the recovery and deepening of democracy."[86] We can choose between "democratic socialism," "eco-socialism," "liberal socialism" (in reference to Bobbio), or, equivalently, "according to specific trajectories involved," "associative democracy," or even "participatory democracy."[87] Suffice it to say, it can disappear without much inconvenience. All in all, Mouffe's "trajectory" is indicative of a new social-democratic common sense.

It may seem to readers that this chapter, centered on criticizing Chantal Mouffe's thought, deviates a bit from this book's general approach. In fact, the argument is of the same nature as those developed in the preceding chapters devoted to the party-form. Historical communist parties, both in one-party systems or conceived as parties among others, were based on an erroneous representation of a monolithic dominant class, assimilated to capital.

We have seen how Gramsci and Althusser managed to distance themselves from this traditional vision, though without shedding much light on the other pole of class domination, "the competent," nor on the necessity for common people to determine their political practice and mode of organization so as to engage in an *alliance-struggle* with the competent. In Laclau and Mouffe's works, there is not only a "hole" in the structure of modern society; the very idea of social structures disappears, along with the issue of their reproduction. As a result, the very coordinates of popular politics disappear. Leaders, whose discourse governs the discordance of popular expectations, thus become a formidable machine for swallowing, obliterating, and making people forget social structures (class-nation-gender) all together—even when, paradoxically, they make the reversal of these social structures the very theme of their discourse. Therefore, we must expect that "movements" are likely to obscure the reality of domination, particularly that of the competent.

It therefore seems the time has come to search for an "alternative" form of political-ecological practice. However, I cannot embark on this path without first presenting in the right order the approach, so far mentioned in bits and pieces, that I believe is required to do so. This will be the subject of the next chapter.

## Notes

1 It seems significant to me that this chapter has been well received in the countries that are most directly concerned, since it has already been published in advance in Spanish, Italian, and Brazilian Portuguese. See Jacques Bidet, "Las visiones de Ernesto Laclau y los trucos de Chantal Mouffe," *LOGOS Revista de Filosofía* 135 (07/21 2020); Jacques Bidet, "Le visioni di Ernesto Laclau et gli stratagemmi di Chantal Mouffe," *Consecutio Rerum* 13, no. 1 (2023); Jacques Bidet, "As visões de Ernesto Laclau e as artimanhas de Chantal Mouffe," *Crítica Marxista* 54, no. 1 (2022).

2 In France, these various possibilities coexist, encouraged by the presidential structure of the constitution. See the Appendix.

3 Ernesto Laclau and Chantal Mouffe, *Hegemony and Socialist Strategy: Towards a Radical Democratic Politics*, 2nd ed. (London: Verso, 2001). In the preface to the French edition published in 2009, Étienne Balibar convincingly develops all the good that can be said of this book. The examination of the subsequent writings of these authors leads me, as we will see, to take the opposite point of view.

4 Ernesto Laclau, *On Populist Reason* (London: Verso, 2005), 86.

5 Laclau, *On Populist Reason*, 86.

6 Laclau, *On Populist Reason*, 110.

7 Laclau, *On Populist Reason*, 68.

8 Laclau, *On Populist Reason*, 85.

9 Laclau, *On Populist Reason*, 97.

10 Laclau, *On Populist Reason*, 85.
11 Laclau, *On Populist Reason*, 170.
12 Laclau, *On Populist Reason*, 95.
13 Laclau, *On Populist Reason*, 76, 87.
14 This is a secular take on theology. The god we are missing, whose absence was once signaled by the tetragrammaton YHWH, who is good, fearsome, merciful, just, etc., is evoked just as well by this or that term of a long "equivalential chain": the Eternal, the Almighty, the God Most High, the Lord, etc. Each of his names evokes and contains all the others.
15 Laclau, *On Populist Reason*, 89.
16 Laclau, *On Populist Reason*, 100.
17 Chantal Mouffe, *For a Left Populism* (London: Verso, 2018).
18 Mouffe, *For a Left Populism*, 11, 26–27.
19 French readers will wonder: Was "social democracy" behind the struggles of 1936–1938 and the implementation the National Council of the Resistance's political program, not to mention the Resistance itself? Should we call "social democracy" the deeply left-wing forces that, from 1945 to 1947, led the "French model" to triumph, combining nationalizations and "social security?" Same thing for the more diverse forces that, to support this model, carried out the strikes of 1947 and 1948, at the high cost of repression? What about the radical plurality that animated the May 1968 movement and the fruitful decade that followed? Was it insignificant that the people seized upon a program that, among other things, nationalized the banks and major industries, abolished the death penalty, prohibited the criminalization of abortion, etc.? And what about, above all, the anti-colonial struggles across three continents, Latin America, Asia, and Africa? They mark the unity of a time when "the air was red," although the North/South contradictions were also prevalent. Chantal Mouffe focuses on her real subject, the people of the North, in Western Europe. But, within this limit, what right does "social democracy" have to appropriate this treasure trove of history and legend? Was all this nothing other than "compromises" and arrangements between capital and labor? In Chantal Mouffe's recollection of this tumultuous mid-twentieth century, the air was rather gray, as evidenced by this final, nostalgic observation: "As a compromise between capital and labour, it allowed a sort of uneasy coexistence between capitalism and democracy." Mouffe, *For a Left Populism*, 26.
20 The danger to be feared by elites, Mouffe explains, came from "the new social movements" and the parallel "wave of labour militancy." Mouffe, *For a Left Populism*, 27. Follow my gaze, she seems to say... Indeed, it was all of this together, but it was inseparably intertwined with older, powerfully resilient social and political dynamics (which the author apparently does not recollect) that constituted the popular strike force of the 1960s and 1970s.

21 Mouffe, *For a Left Populism*, 18 (emphasis added). Does this mean that these parties were actually capable of "giving back to the people the voice" that had been confiscated from them, or only of "presenting themselves as" such? The first interpretation cannot be ruled out, since, to slow down their rise, it is necessary to "recognize that many of the demands articulated by right-wing populist parties are democratic demands." Mouffe, *For a Left Populism*, 21.
22 Mouffe, *For a Left Populism*, 12.
23 Here again, French reader might wonder: Have there not been significant struggles, deeply anchored on the left, against neoliberalism in France over the past 30 years, where the government was defeated over their plans for higher education, pensions, employment, and social security, as well as the European Treaty? Of course, these were only temporary victories. But they put into action hundreds of thousands of political beings involved in the multifaceted world of unions, associations, movements, etc. Doesn't this leave a trace?
24 Mouffe, *For a Left Populism*, 19.
25 Mouffe, *For a Left Populism*, 5.
26 Mouffe, *For a Left Populism*, 18–19.
27 Mouffe, *For a Left Populism*, 60 (emphasis added).
28 Mouffe, *For a Left Populism*, 60.
29 Mouffe, *For a Left Populism*, 61.
30 Mouffe, *For a Left Populism*, 6.
31 Mouffe, *For a Left Populism*, 9.
32 See Chantal Mouffe, *The Democratic Paradox* (London: Verso, 2000); Chantal Mouffe, *On the Political* (New York: Routledge, 2005); Íñigo Errejón and Chantal Mouffe, *Podemos: In the Name of the People* (London: Lawrence & Wishart, 2016).
33 Mouffe, *For a Left Populism*, 92.
34 In *The Democratic Paradox*, Chantal Mouffe develops the idea that "a *well-functioning* democracy requires a vibrant clash of democratic political positions"—i.e., between competing political "forms," associated with different "values" and "passions." Mouffe, *The Democratic Paradox*, 104 (emphasis added). It is also in this *functionalist* spirit that, in *For a Left Populism*, she writes that political parties "provide symbolic markers allowing people to situate themselves in the social world and to give meaning to their lived experiences. In recent years, however, … parties have lost their power to play a symbolic role… . It is [therefore] urgent to *restore* the agonistic dynamics constitutive of a vibrant democracy… . The remedy does not lie in abolishing representation but in making our institutions more representative. This is indeed the objective of a left populist strategy." Mouffe, *For a Left Populism*, 56–57 (emphasis added). These are very odd claims for someone who presents herself as

a proponent of radical democracy. Without a doubt, "the people" must give themselves political organizations capable of "representing" them, provided we give appropriate meanings to these terms. But can we believe that "parties" have the function (the "role," she writes) of enabling individuals to understand how they "situate" themselves in society, and to "give meaning" to their lives? It would seem that, contrary to a functionalism that attributes such a "role" to them, right-wing and centrist political organizations typically aim to blind people to their place in the world and to where the world is headed. Light remains to be shed on parties classified as left-wing. Chantal Mouffe, who has left-wing opinions, considers the right-wing insights to be quite misleading. She therefore works to beat the right. But, in her view, this objective is inseparable from a different, more essential one: the (re)construction of a "frontier" between the left and the right that ensures both antagonistic confrontation and peaceful coexistence between the parties involved.

35 In their preface to the second edition of *Hegemony and Socialist Strategy*, Laclau and Mouffe put forward a new "ontology": "a notion of the social conceived as a *discursive* space." Laclau and Mouffe, *Hegemony and Socialist Strategy*, x (emphasis in original). For them, the "materiality" of discourse is expressed in practices and institutions, but it is indeed "the discourses that constitute the social fabric." Laclau and Mouffe, *Hegemony and Socialist Strategy*, xiii.

36 Mouffe, *For a Left Populism*, 62.

37 It is notable that Laclau and Mouffe never make the slightest use of *Capital*.

38 See Laclau and Mouffe, *Hegemony and Socialist Strategy*, 153 *et seq*. on the topic of "the institution of the social." We must understand that the "social" is something politically instituted. In *On the Political*, it appears to be split in half, since we can read: "The frontier between the social and the political is essentially unstable and requires constant displacements and renegotiations between social agents." Mouffe, *On the Political*, 18.

39 Mouffe, *For a Left Populism*, 88.

40 Mouffe, *For a Left Populism*, 88.

41 Mouffe, *For a Left Populism*, 88.

42 Mouffe, *For a Left Populism*, 88.

43 Mouffe, *For a Left Populism*, 88. As she writes elsewhere, "Things could always be otherwise and therefore every order is predicated on the exclusion of other possibilities." Mouffe, *On the Political*, 18. Yes, of course. But it seems to me that there are social modes of reasoning that are imposed on individuals. There are historical trends indicating that things could certainly change, but not in any particular direction.

44 It's worth noting that, in the work of Laclau and Mouffe, the Great Antagonism between the People and Power is, despite everything, quite

resistant, implicitly drawing a sort of *generic ontology* common to any society where the dominated face a dominant power. It is in this sense that Laclau evokes, in quasi-Freudian terms, the "original scene" where we can see the mass of bearers of "unsatisfied demands" facing "an unresponsive power." Laclau, *On Populist Reason*, 86. As he also writes, "populism requires the dichotomous division of society into two camps"— "the popular camp," which claims "to be the whole," and the other, designated as that of "power." Laclau, *On Populist Reason*, 83. All in all, Laclau and Mouffe borrow alternately from two registers, that of eternal politics and that of the populist moment. But eternalism and momentism, one representing the universal and the other the singular, conspire to repress the particular, i.e., the specificities of modern society, its class structure, and the world-system configuration, which reformat the forms of both patriarchy and "racism." This proclamatory, almost Promethean formulation of the populist gesture, which demands that society be divided into two camps, makes us forget that this division already exists. By reducing the Great Antagonism to the register of "the political," Laclau and Mouffe feed an indifference to the "objective" nature of the social order considered. They reduce what *is* to what *is demanded*, on both sides. Such is the content of this "ontology" according to which society is structured like a language.

45 Mouffe, *For a Left Populism*, 88–89.

46 Mouffe, *For a Left Populism*, 88. Here she seems to have in mind a Marxist approach, although Marx is well known for opposing social positions "in-themselves," i.e., "objective" positions within a social structure, to the forms of "identification" of the subjects "for-themselves"—thus engaging a critique of the objective/subjective pair.

47 Mouffe, *For a Left Populism*, 89.

48 Mouffe, *For a Left Populism*, 88.

49 Mouffe, *For a Left Populism*, 89.

50 Mouffe, *For a Left Populism*, 89.

51 Mouffe, *For a Left Populism*, 89.

52 Mouffe, *For a Left Populism*, 22.

53 Mouffe, *For a Left Populism*, 60.

54 Mouffe, *For a Left Populism*, 61.

55 Mouffe, *For a Left Populism*, 88.

56 The collection of texts assembled by Mickaëlle Provost and Marie Garrau testifies to what a "critical phenomenology" can bring to the study of the "experience" of domination. Marie Garrou and Mickaëlle Provost, eds., *Expériences vécues du genre et de la race: pour une phénoménologie critique* (Paris: Éditions de la Sorbonne, 2022). But can we leave aside the experiences of class and nationality, which are so closely intertwined with those of gender and race? Can we limit ourselves to understanding "social relations" as "experiences?"

57 Mouffe, *For a Left Populism*, 74.
58 Mouffe, *For a Left Populism*, 73.
59 Mouffe, *For a Left Populism*, 73.
60 See Jacques Bidet, *A Political Ecology of Common People*, trans. David Broder (New York: Routledge, 2024), 173 et seq.
61 Mouffe, *For a Left Populism*, 50.
62 Mouffe, *For a Left Populism*, 76.
63 Mouffe, *For a Left Populism*, 76.
64 Errejón and Mouffe, *Podemos*, 109.
65 Errejón and Mouffe, *Podemos*, 109.
66 Mouffe, *For a Left Populism*, 70.
67 Mouffe, *For a Left Populism*, 70.
68 Mouffe, *For a Left Populism*, 71.
69 Mouffe, *For a Left Populism*, 71.
70 Mouffe, *For a Left Populism*, 71.
71 She defends "revolutionary reformism," rejecting both the "sterile reformism of the social liberals who only seek a mere alternation in government" and "the belief held by some people on the left that to move towards a more just society, it [is] necessary to relinquish liberal-democratic institutions." Mouffe, *For a Left Populism*, 46, 39. In her conceptual staging, she thus conveniently surrounds herself with two acolytes capable of making it clear that her place is at the center of the show, between, on the one hand, "liberal-democratic theorists," who dream of "a final reconciliation"; and on the other hand, the "extreme left," which considers the capitalist adversary as an "enemy to be destroyed." Mouffe, *For a Left Populism*, 91. The ambition of left-wing populism is not to cancel the conflict, but to pacify it: "to defuse the potential antagonism that exists in *human relations* so as to make human coexistence possible." Mouffe, *For a Left Populism*, 91 (emphasis added). Peace, therefore, even within families.
72 Mouffe, *For a Left Populism*, 92–93.
73 Mouffe, *For a Left Populism*, 93.
74 See Jacques Bidet, *Théorie générale: théorie du droit, de l'économie et de la politique* [General Theory: A Theory of Law, Economics, and Politics] (Paris: PUF, 1999), 401–30.
75 Mouffe, *For a Left Populism*, 92.
76 Karl Marx, *Capital: A Critique of Political Economy*, trans. Ben Fowkes, vol. 1 (New York: Vintage Books, 1977), 152.
77 On this series of questions, see Bidet, *A Political Ecology of Common People*.
78 Mouffe, *On the Political*, 119.
79 Mouffe, *On the Political*, 119.
80 Mouffe, *On the Political*, 119–20.

81 Mouffe, *On the Political*, 120.
82 Mouffe, *For a Left Populism*, 93.
83 Mouffe, *The Democratic Paradox*, 4.
84 Mouffe, *The Democratic Paradox*, 11.
85 Mouffe, *The Democratic Paradox*, 5.
86 Mouffe, *For a Left Populism*, 51.
87 Mouffe, *For a Left Populism*, 51.

## References

Bidet, Jacques. "As visões de Ernesto Laclau e as artimanhas de Chantal Mouffe." *Crítica Marxista* 54, no. 1 (2022): 9–32.

———. "Las visiones de Ernesto Laclau y los trucos de Chantal Mouffe." *LOGOS Revista de Filosofía* 135 (07/21/2020): 113–29.

———. "Le visioni di Ernesto Laclau et gli stratagemmi di Chantal Mouffe." *Consecutio Rerum* 13, no. 1 (2023): 311–39.

———. *A Political Ecology of Common People.* Translated by David Broder. New York: Routledge, 2024.

———. *Théorie générale: théorie du droit, de l'économie et de la politique.* [General Theory: A Theory of Law, Economics, and Politics.] Paris: PUF, 1999.

Errejón, Íñigo, and Chantal Mouffe. *Podemos: In the Name of the People.* London: Lawrence & Wishart, 2016.

Garrou, Marie, and Mickaëlle Provost, eds. *Expériences vécues du genre et de la race: pour une phénoménologie critique*. Paris: Éditions de la Sorbonne, 2022.

Laclau, Ernesto. *On Populist Reason.* London: Verso, 2005.

Laclau, Ernesto, and Chantal Mouffe. *Hegemony and Socialist Strategy: Towards a Radical Democratic Politics.* 2nd ed. London: Verso, 2001. 1985.

Marx, Karl. *Capital: A Critique of Political Economy.* Translated by Ben Fowkes. Vol. 1, New York: Vintage Books, 1977. 1867.

Mouffe, Chantal. *The Democratic Paradox.* London: Verso, 2000.

———. *For a Left Populism.* London: Verso, 2018.

———. *On the Political.* New York: Routledge, 2005.

# 4 The Rainbow of Common People

The general hypothesis guiding this book, the political-ecological hypothesis, is that damages to life arise exclusively from social domination—the decisive term here being "exclusively." Social domination results not only from *class* relations, but also from *gender* relations and "race" relations (or, more strictly, "*nation* relations"). Here we find not only a well-known "triptych," but also its inherent difficulties. If all of this is indeed the case, then *environmental struggles and emancipatory struggles are strictly one and the same thing*. Environmentalism and social emancipation are one and the same fight. All social struggles are environmental struggles; all environmental struggles are social struggles. However, this hypothesis is difficult to establish. It presupposes that we have first identified the various modes of "social domination," their specific environmental impact, and their interrelations. Correlatively, we must also identify the social forces likely to oppose them. The hypothesis also encounters a contradiction between, on the one hand, ecological peril, which only appears clearly from a global perspective; and on the other hand, a process of emancipation that proceeds from the dispersal of "common people" facing various forms of domination.

This chapter comprises two sections. The first ("Beyond the 'Working-Class Party'") is devoted to a critical overhaul of the heritage of Marxism. I propose a broader conceptual framework designed to allow for a realist study of the contemporary social order, and thereby a means of escape from the ruts of the party-form. On this basis, the second part ("The Substantial Unity of Social Emancipation and Environmentalism") puts forward an analysis of the *global*

DOI: 10.4324/9781003512356-5

relationship between ecology and society on the threshold of what I call "ultimodernity."

## Beyond the "Working-Class Party"

As a warning, readers familiar with my most recent writings, especially *A Political Ecology of Common People*, may possibly skip this section, which provides a brief overview of my "metastructural" approach in its most recent developments.[1] Others will find here a set of conceptual elements essential to the understanding of this book.

What, then, is Marxism missing, despite the central role it has historically played in the struggle against capitalism? How is it that, while remaining a theoretical giant, it has come to appear as a political dwarf? In my view, the reason is that it fails to go beyond the limits of what I call "common Marxism." By this I mean a common treasure that more or less serves as a reference to all those who perceive our society in terms of class exploitation and imperialism. In this sense, it is the continuation of Marx's Marxism. It remains my primary source of inspiration. What it lacks, however, in my opinion, is a full appreciation of its theoretical incompleteness and the political inadequacies that result from it. This is obviously a huge problem. Here it will be addressed in relation to the theme of this book, the political practice of the popular class. What common Marxism lacks is an ability to clearly identify, on the one hand, the duality of the dominant class and the unity of the working class; and on the other hand, the nature of the alternative that remains structurally open in the modern form of society. This can only be seen by pushing the class analysis to a higher level—from the structural level to the *metastructural* level that underpins it. The thesis that I defend, in lapidary terms, is that "common Marxism" is Marxism without the metastructure.

### *An Inadequate Conception of Modern Class Structure*

Let us resume the analysis starting with Althusser. He argues, as we have seen, that it is not enough to destroy capitalist property. Another struggle is necessary, which must begin today. He says it is the task of the "popular masses" to aim for a democracy generalized to the entire social body. But, he adds, this involves "alliances." It remains to be seen with whom and on what basis—assuming we have already identified these "popular masses." The notion of alliance implies that there are potential adversaries of which we can make partners. But common Marxism, which Althusser adheres to, has no analytically constructed concepts by which to designate them. This is not without practical consequences. I must therefore return to the thesis I put forward in the introduction to this book. The dominant class has two poles: capital-power, which Marx analyzes correctly, and "competence"-power, which authors like Bourdieu and Foucault give us some idea of. This "competence" is not to be confused with *knowledge* as such, which is variously dispersed throughout the social body. It concerns the forms of knowledge (and of non-knowledge, blindness, or self-deception, covering things that "competence" cannot or does not want to know) to which social *power* is linked, structurally and institutionally. It can be *attributed* and *received* in the form of diplomas or other signs of recognition and affiliation. Against competence, as we will see, other forms of knowledge, which have a completely different social basis, can be mobilized.

Capital-power is a *power within the market* that enables you to buy and sell, hire and fire, borrow, invest, etc., and thereby make a profit. By contrast, as Foucault has clearly shown, competence-power is a *power within an organization* that decides on the division of tasks; determines the space and time of work processes; defines standards, levels of knowledge, stages, and tests; includes and excludes, etc. These two poles of the ruling class constantly interfere with each other. One is relatively prevalent in the capitalist private sector. The other tends to prevail in the public sector, persisting even when, as in the USSR, capital-power has disappeared. This bipolarity can be observed from protomodernity to ultimodernity (a term yet to be defined), an era into which we have entered.[2]

The difference between these two poles lies in the fact that capital-power is exercised almost silently, at least beyond the relatively closed circuit of corporate shareholders and advertising rhetoric, which is pure instrumentation. Competence-power, by contrast, is obliged at every moment and at every level, including when it is exercised through police violence, to *justify itself* in terms that can be admitted as rational and reasonable. Thereby, even when it seeks to limit information, it is forced to expose itself. Capital-power communicates; competence-power can only be exercised by *communicating about itself* in one way or another. As a result, despite its insertion in capital-power, which calls it to its service, competence-power maintains another type of relationship with the fundamental class. A relative proximity is necessarily established between, on the one hand, certain strata of the "competent," who aspire to free themselves from the yoke of capital, and who are constantly recomposed due to technological changes and economic or political circumstances; and on the other hand, the common people, whom the competent naturally aspire to lead. However, the popular class can only embark on this path through a strategy of cooperation with them that is likely to limit capital-power, as was the case during the era of the social state. Thus, among the competent, certain fractions, notably in the public sector and the scientific and cultural spheres, steer their social power toward a left-wing alliance, while others, notably at the summits of industrial and financial empires, steer it in the opposite direction. Subject to further clarification of the concept of competence, this is what I refer to as the "triangular duel" specific to modern society.

This is how the two complementary yet competing *social forces* that make up the modern ruling class are defined. These are the terms in which a policy of forming bottom-up alliances can be conceived, by which the other class, that of the "common people," aims to promote a union against capital-power with certain fractions of competence-power. Depending on whether capital-power, competence-power, or popular power prevails, it seems relevant to speak respectively of "liberalism," "socialism," or "communism"—such is the terminology I propose. These are, in fact, the three major hegemonic perspectives that oppose each other in modern society. As for "Marxism," the *doctrine* that supposedly aims at communism, it has only appeared as a historical *political force* in the context of alliances between popular forces and certain "competent" forces that are necessary to confront capital-power. Historically, it has been an unstable compromise between "communism" and "socialism," in the sense I give to these terms. Its discourse revolves around class unity, even though it signals an *interclass alliance*. Yet, nothing can arise *to the left* of Marxism because without such an alliance, no power can stand up to capital.

The *class* structure is obviously not the whole of the political configuration inherent in the modern form of society, in which other social relations intervene, notably gender relations and "race" relations—or rather, relations between *nations*, as we will see later. Class relations must nevertheless be considered in their own right. This is what Marx does in *Capital* when he attempts to "construct the concept" of the class structure, i.e., to define it rigorously, so as to understand modern society in its specific rationales and contradictions. This *conceptual* genesis—which takes place in a progressive movement back and forth between criticism of our empirical knowledge and criticism of previous theorizations—is the only way to gain insight into the *historical* development of concrete modern societies. But this social ontology, which aims to define our "social being," should be taken in a way that differs from that of *Capital*, where modern class domination appears as the sole domination of a capitalist class. In reality, it is a dual domination because it is based on two primary social relations,[3] two "class factors": markets and organizations. This duality, articulated under the aegis of a territorial state, defines the "modern class structure" specific to "modernity." These class relations slowly began to appear around the year 1000, in the Europe of the communes (see notably northern Italy) and, even earlier, during the Song dynasty in China. Both of these two "devices," markets and organizations, have existed since much earlier times.[4] But "modernity"—and this is the general hypothesis I am putting forward to define the meaning of the term—emerges when a state is established to articulate the two, asserting itself within a given territory, and gradually imposing itself on the old forms of family, clan, feudal, or state property.

These two "class factors," markets and organizations, constitute a "metastructure" in the very precise sense in which Marx, in Book I, Part One of *Capital*, defines the market as the "presupposition" of the capitalist class structure, as its condition of existence. It is the "metastructural" condition (this is the term I propose[5]) of a class structure that nevertheless "posits" it, i.e., *produces* it as such, by commodifying everything, including labor-power. Marx's error was not to conceive in the same terms the other part of the metastructure, which concerns "competence"-power within organizations. What is traditionally referred to as "capitalism" or so-called capitalist societies results, in reality, from the intertwining of these two class factors into a single, albeit dual, bipolar ruling class. But, to grasp and account for what is involved in this configuration by which these two "class *factors*" come together in the modern "class *relations*," it is necessary to dig deeper and show how the bipolar structuration itself is established.

### *A Blind Spot: The Modern Class Metastructure*

Marx had certainly grasped the problem, but not to the full extent. Already in the *Grundrisse*, he stated that, from now on, two paths were possible, one based on the market and the other on "the organization" (*die Organisation*). At the heart of *Capital*, he thematizes the distinction between the logic of market relations between competing firms, which proceed *a posteriori* by constantly adjusting themselves to supply and demand; and the organizational logic exercised within firms, which adjust their means to ends defined *in advance*. Of course, these two types of logic are constantly intertwined, but they are formally distinct. The reason for this primordial divide is that, beyond "immediate" cooperation through spoken arrangements, only two rational "mediations" (*Vermittlungen*), to used Marx's term, are conceivable: markets and organizations. This theme runs through all subsequent critical political economy, notably American institutionalism.[6] In *Capital*, however, Marx's theoretical development takes a problematic turn, as he treats this duality in historicist terms, exploring how the *competitive logic* of capitalist production, tending toward concentration in ever-larger enterprises, heralds the moment when *organizational logic* will take over, producing an increasingly educated and unified working class capable of assuming leadership. This is how Book I of *Capital* ends. At this point, we supposedly find ourselves at the tipping point where we can see "the pathway" to socialism.

Marx thus gave this great collective "dream" its classical form, known as "communism" throughout the twentieth century. Among others, this was also Althusser's dream. However, it was only possible to give shape to this dream through a *tour de force*, which was also a *sleight of hand* that escaped the gloss of common Marxism. With a little critical attention, we can easily spot it at the very beginning of *Capital*. After having exposed the logic of markets in the first chapter, at the very beginning of the second chapter Marx poses the question of how this logic was established. "Commodities cannot themselves go to market and perform exchanges in their own right."[7] There must be a market to begin with. The "law of markets" is not a fact of nature; it depends, here and now, on human decisions. In this sense, Marx uses the *decisionist* formula: "In the beginning is action." Yet, if we examine the "common," "primordial" action, to use Marx's expressions, we see that it is a "speech act" by which *all* declare their obedience to the law of markets, formulating together a contract of alienation to a strictly market order. The inconsistency of this presentation is that Marx supposes that these modern humans, defined in the first chapter as "free and equal" beings in the marketplace, are not equally capable of freely establishing the rules of *organized* production.

This is indeed the alternative that every modern society gives itself, thus producing its own true "beginning" that is constantly repeated in changing situations. What do modern parliaments debate about? What do adversaries clash over in a class struggle? It is especially what to attribute to the capitalist logic of markets, or to organizational procedures supposedly established democratically, or to direct arrangements between cooperative partners. Therefore, as a sound theoretician, Marx should have begun with this ever-repeating alternative that defines, if not modernity, at least its metastructure. It is only from here that we can understand its structure, with its own historical tendencies and contradictions. This is not "structuralism," i.e., a simple mechanism by which the structure self-reproduces. It is rather a question of *modern* social reproduction, insofar as it is constantly open to an alternative.

The two poles of the ruling class are extremely dissimilar. Marx showed that the logic of capital is ultimately nothing other than that of surplus value, whatever the consequences for humans and nature. To the extent that competence-power is instrumentalized by capital-power, which subordinated it to its interests, as is the case in the age of neoliberalism, it tends to work in capital's service, following the same logic, either within big businesses to sweep away all the forces that try to resist it, or within administrations to subject them to the criteria of profit. Its own logic, however, relates to use-values, within the limits of the advantages it can derive from them. The fact remains that, between the two, competence-power, as Gramsci emphasized, is responsible for promoting consent within the social body. Therefore, it cannot show as much indifference as capital-power to the more or less reasonable nature of the ends pursued, assuming at least that it has not reduced the common people to impotence. Each of these poles has its own mechanisms of *domination*. But also of *exploitation*, for the privileges of competence presuppose, for their very exercise, a lifestyle and therefore a level of income (and of consumption) higher than that of common people—a difference that can only be ensured by a balance of power inherent in the mechanisms of the social reproduction of this domination. Such is the logic of "conspicuous consumption," which is irresistibly reproduced all the way to the bottom of the social ladder. This process of "distinction" is structurally at the heart of the consumerist propensity that, correlatively to the destructive logic of capital, tends to overheat production on a global scale.

Under these conditions, the other class, the one at the bottom, is not simply the "working class," even in the broadest sense of the term. It is the class of the *unprivileged*—who are not powerless, however. This can be seen in the struggles that they have always waged in the realms of property and organizational relations; otherwise, they would remain in *a state of subjection* that the ruling classes reduce them to as soon as the situation lends itself. We can see this today in the conditions of neoliberalism, for an entire segment of the population is subjected to precariousness, colonial capitalist slavery being the most extreme illustration. We owe many great civilizational achievements to the power of this "fundamental class," which has influenced both market and organizational relations: a legally defined working day (the first great workers' conquest), various salary arrangements, the recognition of "qualifications" (distinguished from "competence"), "social rights," etc.; and, regarding the top of the hierarchy within the state apparatus, the conquest of universal suffrage, under the impetus of forces from below. Neither capital-power nor competence-power as such had the slightest interest in any of this. As soon as their prevalence becomes so overwhelming as to define a "regime of hegemony," bot set out to circumvent these popular achievements, either by reducing to a minimum the access of common people to an elective pathway, or by establishing a one-party system. It is only within the framework of "anti-capital" alliances between popular power and competence-power that the "competent" become a partner in democratic initiatives.

### *An Unfinished Theory: The World-System beyond the Class Structure*

There is also another blind spot in Marx's Marxism that was passed on to "common Marxism." The focus was the appropriation of the means of production by a class, but the appropriation of a territory by a community was not theorized with the same acuity. Yet, this is the starting point from which we can understand a *concrete* class configuration. Class structure, in its link to the superstructure, presupposes the appropriation of a territory. Concretely, therefore, *a nation-state is always one among others*, within a whole later theorized as the "world-system," where state and pre-state entities of unequal power confront each other and give rise to asymmetrical relationships. Under these conditions, in the modern era, capital-power tends to cross borders, while "competence"-power tends to operate and organize confrontations within a national space. They are nevertheless in a dialectical relationship of mutual interference, for capital never travels alone, nor do competent conquerors travel without capitalist aims.

This age-old pattern, remodeled from one period to another, prevailed until the turn of the 1970s–1980s, when capitalist forces, engaged in a counter-offensive against the postwar "social state," gradually began to use new communication technologies to weaken this national framework, freeing themselves from the legislation put in place thanks to a certain alliance between the common people and the competent. This technological revolution, which is not to be taken as the cause of this successful bifurcation, nevertheless helped them to achieve their goals: investing in places where the salary is close to zero, keeping research institutes in the center, sheltering income in tax havens, etc. This opened a new era, that of neoliberalism, in which globalized capital-power appears to have inexorably subjugated competence-power. In reality, something like a "world-state" has begun to emerge, intertwined with the world-system that has given rise to state institutions that are not only international, but also supranational, and therefore global.

In its best formulations, the Marxist tradition tends to differentiate between the *state*, which is the "superstructural" articulation of the class structure and the political relations between classes; and the *state apparatus*, which is the functional set of institutions (administrations, treasuries, police forces, etc.) involved in this superstructure, and in which the social classes compete to assert their power within the state. By contrast, "vulgar Marxism" is imbued with an apparently "radical" Proudhonian tradition, which tends to conceive capital and the state as two conniving social forces. In reality, popular struggles are not struggles *against* the state, but *within* the state, to completely change its nature, to "abolish" it as an instance of domination.

The modern state is also something other than a state: it is a *nation*-state. The *modern* form of society is the articulation of markets and organizations *within a territory defined as belonging to a state*. This, among other things, is what makes Machiavelli modern. As Althusser points out, he already thinks of the state as a class state, in the form of a circumscribed territory capable of being defended by an indigenous "common people." It is in this lineage that Gramsci, as a thinker of the Italian *nation*, conceives the question of the social forces required to generate "consent" around a popular project within a national territory. Consider, for example, the Chinese Communist Revolution. While on the Marxist side one tends to see it essentially as a process of revolutionary anti-feudal and anti-capitalist class emancipation that ultimately went wrong, Western observers see it above all as a *national* resurrection that put an end to imperialist influences and paved the way for a *national* return to… capitalist normalcy. In reality, these are two aspects of the same process: the emergence of a radically *modern* society could only come about through a *national* renaissance. These are not two distinct phenomena, but a single "class-nation" process. The same applies to the new nations in which "wars of liberation" emerged, with varying degrees of success. Modern class confrontations presuppose that the stakeholders involved somehow appropriate the common ground on which they take place. We move from a proto-modern nation-state to a *modern* nation-state when common people, within the framework of a form of citizenship that is supposed to be equally shared among all, come to demand to take part in politics on a defined territory, which is declared to be a common heritage, and whose resources are, officially at least, intended to ensure common life under common control. These are mere "declarations," i.e., *claims* that no citizen-compatriot can publicly challenge. Yet, as such, they are available during class confrontations. And no pathway toward socialism or communism can be outlined outside of a context likely to arouse "national" solidarity.

At this point, the "national" question necessarily arises again, but this time on its ultimate scale, that of the world-nation. It arises in a context that no one had dreamed of, that of a "productive-*destructive*" surge in modern society under the impetus of tendencies specific not only to the logic of capital-power, but also to that of "competence-power" and "systemic" forms of domination that the common people themselves are swept into. The question of social domination seems to fade in the face of that of common survival. From now on, all the old political questions clearly need to be thought of in new terms, especially that of the political practice of common people, who must now face not only the ruling class, but also the environmental disaster it is dragging us into.

## The Substantial Unity of Social Emancipation and Environmentalism

It has become increasingly clear, at least to a growing number of humans, that "capitalism is destroying the planet." Yet, this common formulation is not entirely adequate. We cannot leave it at that. As we have seen, within modern society, social *domination* includes other factors, which have quite rightly come to be understood primarily in terms of a struggle for emancipation from a "triptych of domination." Taking up this hypothesis ("The Political-Ecological Hypothesis"), I propose to show, on the one hand, that it is best formulated in terms of "class-nation" ("race")/gender relations ("The Nation in the World-System, of which 'Race' Is the Product"); and on the other hand, that environmentalism now constitutes the compass for any commitment to this triple struggle ("Environmentalism Is Now the Compass of Emancipation").

### *The Political-Ecological Hypothesis*

In this regard, it is appropriate to reconsider each of the three terms of the triptych.[8] However, I will leave aside here the third component, gender, i.e., social sex. Gender relations are closely linked to those between classes and nations (and especially "races"), through multiple overdeterminations. Within the "fundamental class" of common people, "race" and "gender" are intimately present.[9] If here, however, I only marginally discuss gender, it is not because it is of less importance.[10] The reason is that this book is limited to a more circumscribed objective that concerns the substantial unity of the "class-nation" couple, in the sense that I have spoken of Althusser's "class-oriented Marxism" and Gramsci's "nation-oriented Marxism." This line of analysis will lead us to the concept of a "world-nation" engaged in a struggle against a world-system and a globalized class-state.[11]

Let's begin with *class relations*. The tasks to which both social-environmental science and the global environmental movement are dedicated, in the face of the irreversible tipping point that threatens us in the short term, primarily concern capital as such. The term "Capitalocene," as opposed to "Anthropocene," accurately expresses the following thesis: Capital, not "mankind," is what is destroying nature. Marx was the first to clearly demonstrate that the logic of *capital* is, ultimately, that of *profit*, with no regard whatsoever to its effects on humanity and the planet. It is not the logic of *use-values*, of the "good life." In my view, this is indeed an essential point. As I assume that readers know this, I do not intend to return to this subject. Instead, I will confine myself to the other side of the question, which is most often considered only obliquely.

As I have shown above, there is a second facet to modern class domination. This can only be brought to light by crossing Marx's analysis with those of Foucault ("knowledge-power") and Bourdieu ("cultural capital"). This overdetermination significantly alters the content of these two concepts, which are post-Marxian but need to be recycled in a Marxian sense. "Competence," as we have seen—but we must constantly return to this point—must in no way be confused with "knowledge." It is a form of knowledge (and non-knowledge) to which power is attached. Regarding this second aspect, there is a relation of exploitation that is related, not to capital-power, but specifically to "competence"-power, as I have defined this concept. This implies a certain "lifestyle," i.e., level of consumption, that is unrelated to functional necessities (a surgeon could work just as efficiently with a salary close to that of a nurse). Rather, it is related to the balance of power inherent in the cohesion of this superior social power, endowed with the self-reproducing privileges of "competence." This form of exploitation may seem minimal compared to the exploitation carried out by capital-power, which creates an abysmal gap between common people and the financial elite, while at the same time driving the race toward an ecological abyss.

To understand this properly, we must consider the fact that "competence"-domination is not just an external relationship to a "dominated class." It has its own internal dynamic, which is not that of competition (*concurrence*) between capitalists, but that of competition (*compétition*) between the "competent" in a struggle of a hierarchical nature.[12] This is how "consumerism," which capital calls for in its never-ending tendency to *produce-for-profit* (for *surplus-value*), is boosted by an impulse to *produce-to-produce*, i.e., to *produce-for-use* (in other words, to produce supposed use-values, which may well involve social-environmental misuse). These "competitors" seek to prevail over one another, striving to distinguish themselves on two levels: in the eyes of upper management, through the greatness of the projects they prove capable of putting forward (in harmony with the expectations of capital); and throughout the social hierarchy, by ably fulfilling the privileged social functions that are socially attributed to them. Thus, because this "distinction" presupposes a certain lifestyle, i.e., a certain level of consumption, competence-power nurtures a hierarchical consumerist impulse, which results in a hierarchy of incomes.[13] Of course, this consumerism exists throughout society.[14] There are "distinctions" between various strata within the population, depending on the various power relationships they have been able to establish in relation to the dominant class. Meanwhile, the poor masses still must consume more and more to clothe their children in such a way that they are *not* singled out.

Consumerism is therefore not a uniform product of society. It comes from above, not only from the profligate use of dividends, but also, on a wider scale, from the hierarchical form of "competence"-power and the power and prestige attached to it. These are the conditions in which consumerism is constantly recycled. "Common Marxism" structurally tends to obscure this. Such is its ecological weakness, which stems from a deficiency in its social analysis. This is because it expresses a form of historical *compromise* between popular power and "competence"-power. This is also what is obscured by the Marxist formulation "capitalism destroys nature." What is thus amalgamated as "capitalism," and which is actually *the modern form of class domination*, includes two poles based on the two modalities of modern class power, capital and "competence," both of which contribute in their own way to the ecological impact.[15]

In short, it is not in "mankind," in human nature, that we will find the actual mechanisms of nature's destruction. Only the analysis of historically determined social relations of domination and competition, the effects of which are tangible, can enlighten us. These processes are certainly very old, but they have become incomparably more powerful with the developments of modern industrial production. If this is so, we must also analyze the ecological scope of modern struggles for emancipation. Having dealt with this subject in *A Political Ecology of Common People*, I will confine myself here to a few formulations that indicate how one must consider the three elements of the "triptych" of emancipation. The first element is the "structural" struggle (in the class *structure*) of common people, which is a dual process: on the one hand, the struggle of *organizations* against the destructive market forces of capital-power; on the other hand, the *democratic impulse* against the organizational productivism of competence-power. The second element is the "systemic" struggle (within the world-*system*) of the peoples of the South, prey to widespread extractive forces that only their national resistance can counteract. Feminist struggles are the third element. These struggles are environmentalist in themselves, even if this is not always their motivation. By attacking male power in the making of "competencies," they are particularly committed to combating the environmental misdeeds associated with hierarchical powers. These, I repeat, are just a few suggestive indications of a vast program, to which I have devoted greater explanations elsewhere.

### *The Nation in the World-System, of which "Race" Is the Product*

Let us focus for a moment on the second element of the triptych, which is presently the subject of bitter controversy. Speaking in terms of "nation relations" instead of "race relations" may come as a surprise. Yet, it should be self-evident. Modern class relations presuppose a state power whose distinctive feature, in contrast to the premodern era, is that it is established not over a defined population (as was generally the case in the past), but over a clearly circumscribed territory. From here forward, an unstable relationship is established between organizational "competence"-power, which is exercised within national borders (unless it is aimed at pushing them back), and market-based capital-power, which also tends to cross them.

This modern territorial space is "national" only insofar as the fundamental class of common people takes part in its collective appropriation in the form of a nation-state. The emergence of modern nations therefore concerns "state spaces" governed by modern class relations, under the metastructural conditions of *supposed* liberty-equality, which are constantly presupposed and "*posed*" (produced), and by which the power (*potentia*) of those below can be heard. Between various nation-states, however, there are certainly international maxims of peaceful cohabitation, depending on a certain balance of power between them, but without any such metastructural presuppositions. This is why they find themselves in a state of war, real or potential. War has existed since ancient times, waged by the strongest peoples against the weakest. But modern war, in the military-industrial era, is incomparably more destructive and nourished by cooperation between capital-power and competence-power, which seize the opportunity to procure respectively additional "primitive appropriations" and higher distinctions. To the extent that common people declare that they share the eminent property of the national territory, the ruling classes tend to drag the entire nation with them. At the heart of modern history is therefore a radical contradiction between two correlative phenomena: on the one hand, the factual existence of nations as enclosures in which class violence is structurally curbed by popular-class power, whose axiom is that national wealth is common to all compatriots; on the other hand, the factual existence of a plurality of nations, by which foreigners are defined as real or potential enemies, and their territories, as targets to be invaded and plundered if they are in a position of weakness. This is the social-ecological contradiction of modern nations, for better or worse.

"Nation relations" within the world-system are what allow us to understand "race" relations, which in the historical sequence are their indefinitely re-excavated trace and reopened wound.[16] For people of "color," the past lasts a long time, returning in dreams and insomnia. The term "race," assigned to the second term of the triptych, is therefore perfectly justified, even if we know that "races" do not exist, except as social constructions. It designates a truly inhuman form of discrimination. It expresses an experience that is not just that of class and gender violence, but that of a radical denial of humanity. Racism cannot be reduced to relations between individuals, as the methodological individualism of today's analytical philosophy would have it.[17] We know that it inscribes into the present an entire global history. Yet, this past must be analyzed in terms of unequal social relations between *nations*, and especially between nations and non-nations, predating the age of nations. Racism can therefore only be understood in terms of "nation relations," expressing and realizing a nation's power to kill, exterminate, and plunder. "Racism," however, is linked to the world-system only in the last instance, for in its concrete effectiveness it is overdetermined by class and gender relations of exploitation-domination, to which it adds a weight of enslavement and dependence. Therefore, it cannot be fought by isolating it from these other social relations, by focusing for example on a "Black versus White" divide. Immigration is inseparable from a process of integration of Africans into the popular class in its most exploited and most precarious strata.[18]

Linked to a *history of colonization* that is still underway in different forms, racism lends itself to a process of "essentialization" that enables political and social marginalization, perpetuating an ever-revived status of *foreigner*. Today, this is particularly evident in the realms of culture and religion, which secretly maintain, despite denials, the indefinite social reconstruction of the perception of physical appearances, be it skin color or any other trait. This is why it also gives rise to specific struggles for emancipation that are linked to a specific form of pride, that of the "race" reclaimed as such, or of "culture" valued as a contribution to human universality. The environmentally destructive potential of contemporary "racism," understood as a continuation of colonial enslavement by dominant nations, manifests itself in two ways: on the one hand, in the unbridled "extractivism" in territories recolonized by neoliberalism; on the other hand, in the assignment of the poorest populations, deemed more or less "foreign," to dangerously abandoned zones in the Metropoles, notably those affected by the chemical industry or major river and port infrastructures, where the conditions for the existence of racism are reproduced. Just like the anti-neocolonial struggle, the anti-racist struggle against these unsanitary "enclosures" has a positive environmental impact. As we can see, it is indeed the "nation," insofar as it lies at the articulation between the modern class *structure* and the world-system, that allows us to account for "race." It is therefore hardly surprising that the joint task of environmentalism and emancipation is to be understood as the ultimate "national" task, that of a "world-nation"—a concept yet to be defined.

### *Environmentalism Is Now the Compass of Emancipation*

Let's start with the decline of "red" as the symbol of class emancipation. Before the turning point of the 1970s–1980s, the world economy was articulated within an imperialist space. The "national" dimension nevertheless prevailed, and a rather positive relationship, albeit to varying degrees, between a fraction of the competent and the common people was maintained in the wake of the "social state" and various wars of liberation. At this historical turning point, stimulated (which does not mean "generated") by the emergence of new communication techniques, the neoliberal era began. Anglo-American capital, incarnated by Thatcher and Reagan, launched the offensive; then from 1983 onward, it was actively taken up by French socialists who popularized economic deregulation on a global scale.[19] As a result, the old structural configuration specific to modern society, which remained "bipolar" in the sense of an articulation between markets and organizations within a state's territory, tended to metamorphose: "competence"-power, escaping the relative attraction that popular power could exert on it in a national context, became enmeshed in the globalized dynamic of capital. "Red," left to its own devices, was progressively marginalized. On a global scale, the world-system has been recycled in the context of an emerging world-state, under the growing prevalence of capital-power. These are the structural and systemic conditions for a dizzying acceleration of ecological drift. This has irresistibly come to the center of the common concern of humans, since what matters here is not only the domination of some people over others, but also the conditions for the survival of all those who come after us and for the persistence of life in general. From now on, the common *passion* of the human species, which all people can share, can only be the defense of nature.

This is the starting point from which all political and social struggles of common people must now be considered. It is no longer from the point of view of rights, formal or real, to be put forward and obtained, but rather from the point of view of *life* in common—common to all of humanity and to all living beings. This is now the only real adventure available to humans. Not the "mastery" of nature, but, more modestly, more trivially, its preservation. It excites our cognitive powers just as much, whether we are engaged in the expansion of the natural sciences or a new conception of the social sciences, in local experimentation or the renewal of philosophical questioning. It can only take shape through universal cooperation. It calls for initiatives in which everyone can take their part, linking the most modest local initiatives to major collective movements and scientific breakthroughs.

This is the confrontation in which "red" tasks take shape. Struggles to protect forests, soils, sea floors, air purity, etc.—which can take the form of a range of products to be banned, zones to be defended, etc.—are what reveal the social forces that threaten nature. "Green" is therefore the flag of the "final struggle" to overcome the challenge of continuing human history beyond the current disaster. Any social struggle that does not have this environmental horizon is now nothing more than old-fashioned, in hidden collusion with the impulses of the ruling class. This is clearly the task of the youth, called upon to survive in times of disaster, and even more so the task of those who are already presently experiencing it, notably in postcolonial situations subject to the most brutal forms of extractivism. But it is also the task of all humans, who are now able to know that we are heading for catastrophe. "Red" loses all meaning if it does not take "green" as its compass. If it does not rise up to adopt an ecological viewpoint that encompasses the global sociopolitical vision conferred by Marxism, it is irrelevant. Red can only be itself by merging with "green."

## Notes

1 See Jacques Bidet, *A Political Ecology of Common People*, trans. David Broder (New York: Routledge, 2024).

2 In this respect, there is indeed a link between Marx's thought and the Soviet system, since *Capital*, whose object is the critique of the "capitalist mode of production," is expressly underpinned by a collectivist project, which seems to aim to abolish both capital and the market. Of course, this is not the whole story. In addition to a profound and truly foundational theory of capitalism, Marx's political thought is subtle and complex, with an express penchant for cooperative forms and federalism, and a manifest passion for radical democracy. We find a dazzling echo of this in a famous passage from the *Critique of the Gotha Programme* where he writes that after the abolition of capitalist property, the "second phase" will begin, directed against "the unbearable subordination of manual labor to intellectual work," i.e., against competence-power. But what is at stake here is the *conceptual* device Marx puts forward in his great work, which gives a reasoned and consistent form to the collectivist culture of the twentieth century.

3 Paradoxically, what Marx calls the "real domination" of capital, as distinct from its initial "formal domination"—which had not yet modified the production mechanisms that had emerged from craftwork, i.e., "rationalization" through the division and recomposition of tasks, from early manufacturing to computerized production—is the hallmark of competence-power. In contrast to what happens today when market relations such as competition are introduced between agents in administrations, industrial capital fed on the rationality of the knowledge-power it found in other spheres of society.

4 Here we recognize the pair put forward by Polanyi, with the difference that, in my view, in the modern era, the third term, which he defines as "reciprocity," is the instance of social "discourse" that the other two terms are confronted with.

5 Here "meta" refers not to a historical *before*, but a structural *above*. There were certainly markets and organizations before the modern era, but it was only when these two rational forms of social coordination were combined under the aegis of a territorial state that we can speak of "modernity."

6 See R. H. Coase, "The Nature of the Firm," *Economica* 4, no. 16 (1937). Oliver Williamson's theory of transaction costs builds on Coase's work.

7 Karl Marx, *Capital: A Critique of Political Economy*, trans. Ben Fowkes, vol. 1 (New York: Vintage Books, 1977), 178.

8 This section reproduces a few elements from *A Political Ecology of Common People*, but in an extremely summarized form that does not have the value of an analytical argument.

9 Here we encounter multiple problems that require further analysis. The overall triptych configuration "class-nation/gender" constitutes a set of concepts that is more difficult to circumscribe into a "unified theory" than the "class-nation" couple alone. This is why the class-nation divide is marked by a hyphen, while the class-nation/gender divide is marked by a slash. For a lengthier discussion on this triptych, see Bidet, *A Political Ecology of Common People*, Preamble and Chapter 1.

10 Bidet, *A Political Ecology of Common People*, 61–63.

11 Behind this reason lies another, which underpins it: Gender cannot be so adequately integrated into the framework of class/nation "unitary theory," which belongs to the cultural sphere, and the metastructural approach must be limited to this sphere. To adequately deal with the issue of gender, we would need conduct a deeper anthropological analysis. Bernard Lahire shows how the nature/culture pair is not an adequate framework for anthropology and the social sciences, for three terms are required: biological/social/cultural. Living beings are not only biological but also social. Class relations are cultural, but gender relations are both social (animal) and cultural. See Bernard Lahire, *Les structures fondamentales des sociétés humaines* [The Fundamental Structures of Human Societies] (Paris: La Découverte, 2023).

12 The French language has two distinct terms that sociologists can use to distinguish between two types of confrontations between individuals: "*compétition*" within organizations, and "*concurrence*" in markets.

13 Let us not forget Gérard Duménil and Dominique Lévy's demonstration that, under the guise of high "salaries," upper management operates a capitalist drain, following the logic of capitalist accumulation. In the case of the USSR, capital having been wiped out, the competent remain surprisingly "poor," since the accumulation of social power, as we have seen, takes place by other means.

14 At the bottom of the scale, in the divide between people A/people B, this plays out negatively when, for example, poor families can no longer provide their children with clothing symbols (Nike, etc.) that testify to their belonging to the supposed "middle class."

15 Sociological research demonstrates the relationship between "inequalities" and pollution. See Lucas Chancel, *Unsustainable Inequalities: Social Justice and the Environment*, trans. Malcolm DeBevoise (Cambridge, Massachusetts: The Belknap Press of Harvard University Press, 2020). Metastructural theory, which can adopt this analysis, gives it a deeper dimension, showing that these inequalities must be understood in terms of exploitation.

16 For an analysis of the singular case of antisemitism, see Jacques Bidet, *L'État-monde: libéralisme, socialisme et communisme à l'échelle globale: refondation du marxisme* [The World-State: Liberalism,

Socialism, and Communism on a Global Scale. Rebuilding Marxism] (Paris: PUF, 2011), 174–76.

17 For some good examples of this approach, see Magali Bessone and Daniel Sabbagh, eds., *Race, racisme, discriminations: anthologie de textes fondamentaux* (Paris: Hermann, 2015).

18 Florian Gulli has demonstrated that there is a "liberal anti-racism" that prides itself on the success of an elite of color, and whose success lies in the interest that the ruling class has in separating supposedly cultural "race" relations from the relations of exploitation and marginalization with which they are intimately linked. See Florian Gulli, *L'antiracisme trahi: défense de l'universel* [Anti-Racism Betrayed: Defending the Universal] (Paris: PUF, 2022).

19 On the neoliberal turn in France and its international consequences, see Rawi Abdelal, *Capital Rules: The Construction of Global Finance* (Cambridge, Massachusetts: Harvard University Press, 2007).

## References

Abdelal, Rawi. *Capital Rules: The Construction of Global Finance.* Cambridge, Massachusetts: Harvard University Press, 2007.

Bessone, Magali, and Daniel Sabbagh, eds. *Race, racisme, discriminations: anthologie de textes fondamentaux*. Paris: Hermann, 2015.

Bidet, Jacques. *L'État-monde: libéralisme, socialisme et communisme à l'échelle globale: refondation du marxisme.* [The World-State: Liberalism, Socialism, and Communism on a Global Scale. Rebuilding Marxism.] Paris: PUF, 2011.

———. *A Political Ecology of Common People.* Translated by David Broder. New York: Routledge, 2024.

Chancel, Lucas. *Unsustainable Inequalities: Social Justice and the Environment.* Translated by Malcolm DeBevoise. Cambridge, Massachusetts: The Belknap Press of Harvard University Press, 2020.

Coase, R. H. "The Nature of the Firm." *Economica* 4, no. 16 (1937): 386–405.

Gulli, Florian. *L'antiracisme trahi: défense de l'universel.* [Anti-Racism Betrayed: Defending the Universal.] Paris: PUF, 2022.

Lahire, Bernard. *Les structures fondamentales des sociétés humaines.* [The Fundamental Structures of Human Societies.] Paris: La Découverte, 2023.

Marx, Karl. *Capital: A Critique of Political Economy.* Translated by Ben Fowkes. Vol. 1, New York: Vintage Books, 1977. 1867.

# 5 Organize, Associate, Rise Up

Conceiving the political *practice* of common people is distinct from conceiving a *program*, for it involves a *different* question, formerly referred to as that of "organization." There is no universal answer to this question. Politics involves the here and now. A political project is only defendable in relation to a specific situation. On the scale of a nation-state, the politics of common people presupposes that the nature of the various social forces at play has been identified. This implies that one must consider the terms of the political constitution (separation of powers, federated or unitary state, etc.), the body of legislation, the administrative structure, the relationship between town and country, the history of class and gender struggles, cultural and religious conflicts, the historical identity of various organizations, the economic and ideological circumstances, etc., as well as the affects that all this together generates. Anyone who proposes a strategy is expected to have at least analyzed the entire set of these elements and to reason in terms of changing local circumstances. However, these situations are linked in multiple ways to global circumstances that immediately affect and concern everyone. Thus, in an age of ecological disaster, a popular strategy only makes sense if it tackles a "here and now" on a global scale. We must therefore go beyond the idea that there are only singular pathways for bottom-up strategies. If it is true, as Gramsci claims, that such an endeavor presupposes a common will in the form of a "nation," this is the concept that must now be questioned. This chapter analyzes it in its dual dimension as a nation-state ("Bottom-Up Political Practice") and a world-nation ("The New International").

From there, as we shall see, in addition to the centuries-old popular practices of organization and association, a new form of practice has

DOI: 10.4324/9781003512356-6

emerged that is appropriate for the present time. The term "uprisings," which has been used often recently, is perfectly adequate to the concept behind it. I will therefore take it up here ("The Age of Uprising").

## Bottom-Up Political Practice

Why are large "rainbow" organizations not appearing everywhere, even if a strictly social logic of emancipation seems to call for them? What obstacles do modern class relations, gender relations, and nation relations pose to popular political organization?

In the age of disaster, the class structure of modern society remains as it is, with a bipolar dominant class that combines capital-power and competence-power. The problem is therefore to determine what will become of the "alliance" between common people and a defined fraction of the "competent." We are not entering postmodernity, even less posthistory, but rather "ultimodernity," the ultimate form of modernity, through which *modern* history continues. *Systemic* domination is intertwined with *structural* domination, now increasingly centralized globally. At the same time, in the face of the two *mediations*—market-based coordination and organization-based coordination as factors of social class—the *immediacy of a universal discourse* emerges that bears witness to and is nourished by the action of non-governmental organizations (NGOs) and global environmental institutions, illustrating the potential of a global anti-capital "alliance." The fact remains, however, that the impulse that drives the world of the competent pushes them again and again to take the lead, as can be seen in various "green" movements, even when they have chosen the left. The question of the balance of power between competence-power and popular power has therefore not disappeared.

### *Top-Down Politics and Bottom-Up Politics*

Today, common people can grasp the global character of environmental phenomena, as the media remind them every day (though often in dubious terms). They can therefore also grasp the need for a global response involving all nations in a deployment of shared knowledge and emotions. However, for ordinary people—who are structurally defined as the popular class, the class of the unprivileged—entering politics is particularly difficult. For members of the dominant class, it occurs almost naturally, since their social conditions predispose them to occupy positions of leadership. This is particularly true of the competent (who also tend to take on leadership in the archipelago of associations). The formula "masters and possessors of nature" can be emblematically applied to them, as they spontaneously identify themselves as the designated *protectors* of nature. Common people, by contrast, first encounter politics in a set of local-family social experiences of "modesty." These experiences are circumscribed by a local context of housing, schooling, information, income, and employment conditions that determine the personal future each person can envisage. Individuals' political *identities* are certainly a function of the major events, wars, economic crises, social movements, and migrations they may encounter throughout their existence. But their political *consciousness*, in terms of *class*, *gender*, or *racial consciousness*, is forged in day-to-day confrontations with discrimination and oppression, which they only become "aware" of through a set of collective or associative processes, from urban revolts to union organizing. There is therefore a kind of contradictory tension between the signs that come from global environmental experiences, now common to all humanity, and the signs that emerge from experiences in one's immediate social surroundings. This gaping discrepancy is the starting point from which we must attempt to conceive the political practice of common people.

### *Four Challenges Facing Popular Political Organization*

Four points require our attention. It is tempting to think they mainly concern European countries. However, they refer to more general processes, significant of modernity, that are found to varying degrees throughout the world.

1 *The people A/people B divide.* The first challenge facing popular political unity is the gulf between two fractions of the popular class, which I call "people A" and "people B." "People A" are those who have managed to protect to some extent, or even develop, certain rights and powers they enjoy thanks to the social conquests of the past. "People B" are those who tend to be dispossessed of these rights and powers. This notably includes a greater number of women, people who are racialized or perceived as foreigners, rural people, and young people. Among the symptoms of this worsening social malaise is the fact that these people, facing heightened

discrimination of various kinds, are increasingly experiencing economic and administrative dependency (particularly in terms of knowing and securing the recognition of their rights), job insecurity, housing insecurity, etc.; and are marginalized both socially and politically, participating even less than in the past in electoral processes and traditional political life. This is what needs to be considered in relation to the subject at hand: not the (obviously essential) task of determining what measures should be taken, but, more specifically, the task of investigating what mode of political practice and organization would enable the broadest popular participation in designing and implementing such measures.

2 *Groundedness*. Popular sociopolitical vitality had previously been able to find its most solid ground in large businesses or public-sector organizations, where the professional conditions that generate solidarity tend to reproduce themselves. Today, this reproduction process has become increasingly unstable, due to corporate breakups and relocations, and the rampant privatization eating away at major public services. Revolutionary trade unionism, steeped in politics and capable of disrupting the production process, is the only way to shake the machinery of political domination. Major strikes, even if they alone cannot ensure victory in the long term, have marked the course of modern history. But this does not mean ws are necessarily the right place for the political organization of common people. At the same time—and this is a universal fact—the *fluidity* of digital technology, which is reshuffling all interactive forms of individual and collective communication, has gradually taken on a preponderant role in political, institutional, and informal life. This is not the place to assess the benefits and drawbacks of this. We know how much rulers can use this to their advantage. Sufficc it to say that digital communication technologies also allow common people to reappropriate political discourse, thereby helping them to resist the neoliberal juggernaut. They also tend to create an unprecedented articulation between the explicit "politics" of political parties and alternative, "associative" forms of politics, as well as individuals' commitment to specific issues considered to be part of the common cause. However, since what is at stake here is the construction of a mode of political organization aimed at prevailing nationally over the forces of domination, the question of its groundedness becomes imperative. Local towns and neighborhoods appear to offer particularly "firm ground." This is where people live and often work, and

where they make friends and form couples. It is where they know each other through school, shops, sports venues, leisure activities, local social institutions, etc. In short, this is the *solid ground* on which face-to-face encounters take place.

It is not just a matter of a "phenomenological" privilege by which *local* communities may open the possibility of mutual "recognition." The political power of "place" lies in the fact that it is where the parameters of our social ontology—i.e., our administrative, economic, cultural, and everyday lives—concretely intersect and become an object of politics. Local communities are now, more than workplaces (which are increasingly relocatable), the elementary cell of our "locality," of our social being as "being-in-a-place" endowed with its own social and political heritage. Local communities are also, in essence, a place of meeting, i.e., of confrontation. We know that the rise of remote work, accelerated by the COVID-19 pandemic, has further weakened companies' social fabric and transformed people's homes, which have once again become workshops, into urban links in the political process. Urban sociology shows how privileged populations appropriate and produce (or have produced) excellent neighborhoods for their own use. And, in the present period, dominant powers have continued to *separate* populations in this sense. The fact remains that local spaces, in contrast to the fluid digital space where we communicate with our peers, are where we encounter the most people who are not like us. We are bound to *cohabitate*. Unequally, of course. And it is through the physical space of local communities and their inequalities that people meet their own destiny and must decipher themselves as citizens of a place that is part of a nation, and, ultimately, part of the world as a whole. This is therefore the starting point for the political organization of common people. It may be thought that the local level, particularly based on local elections (as opposed to national ones), is more than ever the scale on which the politics of emancipation can be deployed—even if parts of the population, particularly young people, are increasingly escaping their assigned locality.

3 *Symbiosis between heterogeneous political cultures.* Another challenge is the cohabitation of activists with different political cultures, well beyond what can be apprehended as various "currents." From the early "labor movement" to the present day,

political awareness within the popular left is linked to struggles that are incomparable with each other. The practical memory that emerges from these struggles is nourished by disparate founding events, experienced on a variety of scales, that gave rise and continue to give rise to traditions, stories, legends, heroic figures, principles of analysis, and more or less discordant bodies of doctrine. This results in a multiplicity of political parties, groups that are more or less well-funded and sustainable, and sites of intellectual and emotional affiliation. The form of activism that we label as "political," which aims to prevail within the state apparatus, is only one particular modality that is powerless in itself if it does not aggregate two other equally political forms: "associative" activism, in the common sense of the term (trade unionism being an eminent form); and "selective" activism, in the sense of a lasting or occasional commitment to a specific cause considered to be relevant to social emancipation or environmental protection. This is also what the political organization of common people must take into account.

4 *The main danger.* The main danger facing any "socialist"-oriented popular political project is certainly its tendency toward bureaucratization. As Robert Michels argued in 1914, this gives rise to hierarchy and an elite inclined to take charge. According to my metastructural analysis, however, this tendency originates more fundamentally from the very structure of modern society. It does not come from the common people's "main enemy," capital, but from their potential ally, "competency." This paradox stems from the formidable constraint represented by the dual requirement of both an *alliance* with the competent and a *struggle* against them, insofar as they are not only the functional agents of capital, engaged in "producing for profit," but also agents endowed with their own structural potential for domination and exploitation. When common people gain political power, part of the "competent" population tends to join the ranks of the popular "party." But the same can also happen in a situation of decline, when the political institutions (parties and circles of influence) that federate the "competent" are themselves swept away in disarray. Indeed, some of the "competent" have a structural tropism toward the popular class. Whatever the case, the triangular duel remains a duel, class against class, in which everyone must choose their side, willingly

> or unwillingly. Many, therefore, understand that, rather than being the last under the flag of the ruling class, it is better to carry high the banner of the popular class.

Things are not declared in these terms, as it is a taboo. It is nevertheless a well-known fact. Popular parties therefore face a double jeopardy. On the one hand, they see an elite pouring in from outside, ready to take the lead. On the other hand, as they seek to protect themselves against this through a democratic centralism designed to ensure the pre-eminence of their popular-class members, they tend to produce their own elites, experts in political procedure and united in the process of the party's own reproduction through the very exercise of politics. From this arises the opposite, anti-bureaucratic tendency, formerly expressed in anarchism and now appearing, in contrasting ways, in the alternative "movement" model, the supposed emanation of an indistinct "gray matter" that supposedly self-governs in the name of "Us," down below, and against "Them," up above. Here, the surreptitious emergence of "competent" domination is achieved—by performative denial—under the guise of populism, through the pretension of a horizontality of power in motion, above which rises the figure of the supreme leader, who inspires in turn, by way of mimesis, subordinate tribunes, endowed with an effective rhetorical culture stemming from their cultural heritage, and bound together by the "secrets of the trade." It remains to be seen how common people will be able to concretely confront this double jeopardy, one bureaucratic, the other charismatic, the latter brooding over its own clandestine micro-bureaucracy.

## A New International

Clearly, it is now on a global scale that the "human scale" is to be found. The human community, faced with its problems, "interpellates" each human being as a world citizen.[1] If so, it is on this social and ecological scale that the question of the "organization" of common people arises. In this section, I will naturally draw on the concepts I developed in *A Political Ecology of Common People*.[2] Of particular importance is the structure/system pair, where "structure" is understood in the sense of class and gender structures, and "system," in the sense of the world-system, i.e., a global set of core/periphery countries in their economic, political, military, and cultural dimensions. It is in a "systemic" context, defined in this way, that a process emerged starting with the neoliberal turn of the 1970s–1980s that must be analyzed in "structural" terms (this time referring to a world structure). I call this process the "world-state." By this I do not mean a "global state" in the banal sense of the term, i.e., a state apparatus endowed with its own exclusive republican institutions, immediate citizens, police force, army, etc. I mean a world-state with a class structure similar to that of nation-states, but which, insofar as it unites the human community in its totality, is in a relationship of dialectic immanence with every nation-state—i.e., a relation between the whole and the parts that emerges as the parts increasingly adopt the same neoliberal constitution as a universal supreme law. In these conditions, one can only be identified as a world citizen by first being identified as a citizen of one's own particular nation. The world-state and the world-system thus determine each other reciprocally. However, as humans' capacity to intervene in the natural order develops, for better or worse—especially worse—it is the world-state that encompasses the world-system, and not vice versa. And the worst can only be averted if, against both the world-state and the world-system, a universal revolution emerges whose concept can only be that of the "world-nation." This is what I intend to demonstrate, in any case.

### *The Worldwide Class Struggle in the Age of Disaster*

In a time of disaster, isn't something changing in the relationship between common people and the competent? It is true that the neoliberal world-state continues to assert itself, with "markets" exerting an ever-increasing influence on the global economy. However, if it is true, as Marx argues, that capital has no other logic than profit, we must admit that it does not reign as an absolute master, in the mode of an "absolute capitalism," according to a concept put forward by Étienne Balibar. Indeed, capital encounters social forces that thwart it. The COVID-19 pandemic revealed some fleeting symptoms of its weakening. The institutions of the UN, an essential part of the contradictory conglomerate of the world-state, indeed displayed a certain "positive globality." Television viewers around the world, many of whom were still unaware of its existence, heard day after day about the WHO, which had established itself as the supposed supreme judge of the measures to be taken in the face of danger, including the value of vaccines. A large number of specialists from around the world, including Americans, collaborated with the WHO, even though the United States had withdrawn from it. In this case, the world-state, insofar as it exerts the presence of different peoples through the UN, began to exert some influence on the world-system.

Although this influence is certainly still minimal, the recent High Seas Treaty (2023), which is clearly anti-neoliberal, suggests that it is likely to grow over time, given the ecological challenges. Supranational UN organizations—WHO, FAO, ILO, UNESCO, UNICEF, IPCC, etc.—as well as meetings such as the COP, at least *claim* to set the tone on a world scale. And even if this line is rarely followed, in the face of the power of the capitalist institutions of the world-state and the balance of power within the world-system, such a claim is significant of our "ultimodern" condition. The recent ruling of the International Court of Justice, which for the first time since its creation in 1945 found against a Western state—in this case Israel, accused of genocidal practices—marks a historic turning point. The initiative of the International Criminal Court to target Western political leaders is in the same vein. Something has shifted in the North/South balance. New dynamics have appeared. However, it remains to be seen whether they have the same social potential on the world-state scale as on the nation-state scale—in other words, whether they can be read as precursors of a long-term historical trend.

The global economic situation can be analyzed at the crossroads of structural and systemic factors, each of which overdetermines the other. But it is structural factors, not systemic ones, that determine how the situation tends to develop. The system as such has no tendency other than to reproduce itself in various forms through successive upheavals.[3] *Tendencies arise from structural factors.* And the modern class structure indeed tends to change. But in what way? This was the central, or at least ultimate, objective of the analysis developed in *Capital*, which is a lengthy theoretical investigation into the tendencies inherent in what Marx called the "capitalist mode of production." The diagnosis put forward was that it was evolving toward a breaking point. As organizational (versus market) logic develops in large capitalist firms, and as the workers become ever more numerous, schooled (*geschulten*), and united by the same process, they will end up being able to take control. This is the perspective that Book 1 of *Capital* leaves us with. Marx's mistake, as seen earlier, was to overly rely on this hypothesis, which was unrealistic and ultimately catastrophic. In reality, as we know, markets have continued to develop and have been able to take precedence over organizations.

It is important to note, however, that this is an error of *historical* diagnosis, and not an *epistemological* error, i.e., one that concerns the requirements of a theory of history. In this regard, Marx's guiding conviction—which he has no monopoly on, since it lies at the heart of all historical reasoning—is correct. We can only *begin* to explain and understand the historical process of modernity by proceeding *from the structure to its tendency*. Only then can we pursue the investigation of the *circumstances* (notably systemic wars, pandemics, climate change, etc.) that mark the inherent disorder of the course of history, thwarting the expected trends and evolutions of a given type of society. Such was the case, for example, when the Mayan empire, which the expected course of history seemed to promise a bright material and cultural future, was erased from history by a radical climate change that wiped out its economy and thus all its institutions. This is where, as we've seen, Marx's *theory of structure* is insufficient, inadequate; consequently, his approach to structural *tendencies* is erroneous as well. In reality, the class structure takes the form of a "triangular duel." It is indeed a duel because there are two classes; but it is also triangular because there are three "social forces" that come into play, in variable relationships depending on the two alternative possibilities open to the "competent": an "alliance to the left" (from the years 1935/40 to 1970/80) or an "alliance to the right" (since 1970/80), correlative to neoliberal globalization. The question is whether this balance within the global social order can now be considered stabilized—like the "end of history." Or could this globalized class structure be such that, in the context of disaster, another possible outcome might emerge?

Since the world-state has an immanent relationship with nation-states, we find the same triangular-dual structure. Competence-power participates in the processes of domination and exploitation on both a world scale and a national scale. But it only exists as such to the extent that it *appeals* to common *reason*. And, to this extent, while it exercises "knowledge-power"—mixed with a whole range of *non-knowledge* pertaining to everything it cannot or does not want to know—it is forced to *share* its knowledge. It cannot avoid relinquishing the monopoly of a share of the knowledge that belongs to the exercise of its power. In short, neoliberal globalization does not move beyond modernity. The class structure, both globally and nationally, remains what it is. However, within it, the balance of power has shifted. In the heyday of national social states, common people had become powerful enough to attract the competent into a certain "left-wing alliance," which materialized in vast programs of social legislation, public services, and nationalizations. But, at the turn of the 1970s–1980s, capital-power, insofar as it succeeded in imposing deregulation and financialization, proved capable of overcoming borders, breaking the relative autonomy of nation-states within which popular power had managed to gain enough strength to enable a certain "alliance to the left." As a result, competence-power became subservient to an "alliance to the right."

Now, as we cross the threshold of "ultimodernity"—the ultimate phase of modernity that is being "structured" on a planetary scale and not just on the level of nation-states—a certain reversal of the situation is taking place that is favorable to an "alliance to the left" against capital-power. The basic facts about the impending catastrophe are indeed simple to *understand*, at least once their reality has been publicly established. This is the case with the causes and consequences of global warming, air pollution, land pollution, water pollution, etc. The emergence of a genuine ecological culture, accessible as such to the mass of humanity, gives rise to an unprecedented potential for alliances. Faced with the rise of knowledge that common people have thus acquired, "competence" (which does not mean "knowledge") tends to lose the benefits linked to its monopolistic position, and with it, its overhanging position shared with capital. And this is how it can tend to move from the neoliberal right-wing alliance to a left-wing alliance.

This argument is not a revival of the old idea according to which knowledge, by enlightening common people, will liberate them. It is based on an examination of a change that has appeared, in the age of "ultimodernity," within the "triangular duel" specific to modern society. In this sense, it also runs counter to Bourdieu's reasoning according to which intellectuals have a personal interest in truth and the reputation of truth, and thus in their independence from "temporal" powers. This predisposes them to guide the people. My argument is more realistically grounded in an analysis of the relations of power and reason within modern society. A popular alliance with the competent remains a *struggle*-alliance. From the moment competence-power releases itself from the "abstraction" of capital, that of pure profit, it tends to arrogate to itself the leadership of the struggle against it, taking itself as the source of all conceivable "light." It is no coincidence that green parties first took root in the "upper intellectual strata." As can be seen in the electoral arena, competence-power (once again, not as endowed with knowledge, but as competent authority) spontaneously imagines that, with the ecological disaster, the time for Enlightenment has finally come. For common people, therefore, it will be a matter of engaging in a *struggle*-alliance with and against the competent, right up to the ultimate scale. If at least it is true that the destruction of nature results exclusively from the misdeeds of social domination, the perspective of such an *alliance* tends to become more plausible as the popular class, acquiring more ecological knowledge, finds itself in a better position to advance the universal interests that it alone represents, the interests of life. And this alliance can only be sustained by a global social-environmental struggle whose aim can only be that of a world-nation.

### *The World-Nation against the World-System and the World-State*

One of the most common ways to describe the current situation is to speak of "crisis"—economic crisis, political crisis, demographic crisis, migration crisis, and now climate crisis. Far from enlightening us on the relationship between those phenomena, this piling up of "crises" actually obscures the seriousness of the situation. We are not going through an "ecological crisis," a crisis from which we could emerge after a "transition" that would allow us to return to and ultimately overcome the previous situation, as in the case of economic crises. We are somewhere between disaster and catastrophe. The "disaster" has already begun, for life on earth has already regressed significantly, and it will never again be what it was. However, it seems we have not yet reached the moment of "catastrophe," of general irreversibility, the point from which it would be impossible to stop the process of destruction and envisage any form of repair.

Why, then, in these conditions, should we appeal to the concept of a "world-nation?" Let us remember Machiavelli's lesson. The dominant can only be brought down by the force of the multitude below. And this can only be realized on the basis of a territory circumscribed as a common nation, an eminently common "good," where the stakes of class confrontations, but also gender confrontations and nation confrontations (including "race" confrontations) are *concretely* defined. Earlier we discussed the historical relevance of this proposition, at the crossroads of a class-oriented Marxism and a nation-oriented Marxism, respectively put forward by Althusser and Gramsci. We also discussed its limit; the nation defines a world around itself that is *foreign* to it. And, as we see in the case of the European Union, the super-nation only pushes further away the curse of a deadly border, beyond which there are only enemies and potential intruders. We therefore paradoxically need *a nation without borders*, a *world-nation*. Is this conceivable? And what would be the content of such a concept?

Let's return to the birth of modern nations. At the time of the great European revolutions, the "nations" of *nation*-states came to revolutionize modern states—which had been gradually asserting themselves for centuries—by transforming them into *politically* modern states. This happened when common people openly entered politics, putting forward on their own behalf these doubly amphibological claims proper to all nations: "this land is *ours*"; "it belongs to us *all*"; "it is ours *alone*." Thus, two pretensions were simultaneously proclaimed: the inclusive ambition to be part of a national power shared by all compatriots and, correlatively, the exclusive appropriation by a community of a defined territory. An examination of the very diverse circumstances in which such a process occurred would go beyond the limits of this book. Let us just note that, when proclaimed by common people, the inclusive "nation" targets the "class-nation (race)/gender" dominations that weigh down on them. This is how we should understand the cheer "long live the nation!" that is present in all modern revolutions, even if there is a large gap between proclamation and realization. *Class* emancipation, in the name of "liberty-equality-fraternity," became the horizon of common people's struggles. *Gender* emancipation involved the same demands turned against patriarchal state institutions. As for *national* emancipation, the wars of *national* liberation during the twentieth century asserted themselves as inseparably requiring the equality of citizenship between the members of a people, and the equality of peoples within the world-system. We know that the results are far from satisfactory, but such were the demands that drove this great historical movement. The "nation" was expected to transfigure common people's destiny.

The age of neoliberalism, which is the one where we cross the threshold of ultimodernity—modernity in its ultimate dimension, that of the planet—does not leave behind the "modern social order," i.e., the historically specific articulation between the (modern class) *structure* and the (world-)*system*. However, a state's class logic and gender logic, which are those of the "triangular duel" within the nation-state, tend to be redeployed, as we've seen, on the scale of a world-state. *Yet, it is paradoxically because of the emergence of this world-state that a world-nation is conceivable.* Modern states, established on defined territories, have given rise, under the pressure of popular struggles, to "nations" as common spaces and common goods for fellow citizens—*nation*-states. Nations of solidarity, within the limits of the "triptych of domination," but fragmented, bearing the stigma of the recurring asymmetry within the world-system. It is through a completely different process that the entry into ultimodernity gives rise to an impulse toward a world-nation, i.e., an ambition, potentially shared by all humans, to take charge of the affairs of the human community as a whole. This ambition is driven by the progressive awareness of an ecological peril that threatens us all. In these conditions, as we have seen, a new perspective for a left-wing alliance against the destructive logic of capital is emerging between the "competent," who are taking on new responsibilities, and common people, who are acquiring elementary but decisive ecological knowledge. Indeed, from now on, common *knowledge* encroaches on the prerogatives of *competence*, which cannot communicate without *communicating part of itself*, thus losing the monopoly on data essential to ecological decisions. As soon as this is established, anyone can now roughly judge what needs to be done to slow down global warming, the extinction of species, and sea pollution. It is hardly surprising, therefore, to find that people and populations are the first to come into play.

If, however, we want to understand what the global world-nation process consists of, we must introduce a new, decisive concept: that of *dialectical immanence*, i.e., the reciprocal relationship between the whole and the parts. Understanding the world-nation requires that we begin by considering that the world-state is not simply an overhanging reality. It is not external to nation-states. It is in a dialectical relationship with nation-states, which must not be conceived as "members" of it, but rather as parts of a whole with which they share the same nature.[4] When citizens engage in environmental or social struggles, they are acting as "citizens of the world." These local struggles, accumulating into national achievements, are what give content and consistency to the global balance of gender and class powers. They influence supranational legislation, which, once established, correlatively exerts a positive influence within each nation. The same applies, in the opposite direction, to the advances of capital-power and competence-power, and just as much to gender power. Such is the ultimodern class struggle. The world-nation is the dialectical process between the national parts and the national whole, through which the human community seeks to free itself from class-based, gender-based, and nation-based dominations that threaten the survival of the planet.

This dialectic unfolds on two distinct levels. *Against the world-state*, popular class struggles directed toward the world-nation aim, as they do already on national territories, to subject *markets* and capital-power to public *organization*, and to subject this organization to the democratic demands of free *cooperation* between all "fellow citizens." This is how we can recognize what one might call "the bottom-up strategic axiom," however modest its results may appear. According to such an axiom, the popular class, at the local level, tends to favor nationalized railways over private highways, and to impose thrifty and popular use of and control over the rail network. At the global level, it tends by the same logic to give precedence to the types of institutions of which the UN system gives us an initial idea. Thus, in its emergence, the world-nation faces the dual challenge of creating solidarity in the relations of production, education, and health, and of promoting ecological wisdom. *Against the world-system*, the world-nation faces other challenges. It does not advocate the *abolition* of nations, but rather the support of weaker ones against those that dominate them. Insofar as it exists, it works to promote international legal standards along these lines. In the face of armed violence between nations, however, today's UN can only play a modest role. Beyond a certain threshold, as we know, it finds itself obliged to "entrust the task" to the war machines of systemic core or sub-core countries, which are interested in gaining imperial benefits.[5] Once again, there is only one last resort against warlike violence: that the common people of each nation succeed in moderating it by pushing back the dominant class, especially capital-power, by withdrawing its hold on the state apparatus and state apparatuses.

In short, the "relation of dialectical immanence" between singular nations and the world-nation works upwards and downwards in equal measure. In this incessant back-and-forth movement, in this dialectical pulsation, it remains to be seen in what terms world citizens can conceive their practice.

Here, once again, the question arises: "How do we organize?" But, as it is a matter of conceiving a new mode of popular political practice, is "organization" the best word to use? Let us first clarify the relationship between *organizations* and *associations*, which involve two distinct types of social relations, one marked by a hierarchical order (even in the form of democratic centralism), the other by rules that tend to favor more horizontal power relations. These are two connected but distinct forms of modern political interaction. On the national level, the political order already implies certain kinds of "associations." The dominant parties not only dominate through their hold on the state apparatus, but also through the presence of their members in what Althusser, in the spirit of Gramsci, called "state apparatuses": public or private entities of all kinds where class, "race," and gender relations are crystallized, such as schools, businesses, churches, trade unions or professional associations, sports or cultural associations, etc. People's emancipation parties, whether communist or social-democratic, have similarly included in their programs the need to invest in all of these "apparatuses" by calling on their members to get involved in the appropriate associative networks.

At the end of the nineteenth century, the Social Democratic Party of Germany created a multitude of theatrical, cultural, and sporting associations that orbited around it. By joining a "working-class party" (but the same goes analogically for the "radical left" today), one had to understand that the task immediately required was to get involved, if it wasn't already the case, in associations with prospects for emancipation in affinity with those of the party: parent-teacher associations, tenants' associations, neighborhood associations, cultural associations, and especially working-class trade unions, the most perilous form of commitment. This also meant setting up such associations, and others like them, where they did not already exist. The popular political practice of establishing organizations thus spread to the practice of establishing multiple associations involving more circumscribed objectives, as well as other criteria and modes of action. It was correlatively nourished by this immersion in all spheres of life.

This structural duality of activism, which combines organizational and associative practices, is found on the scale of the world-nation, but it is distributed in a completely different way. Organizational schemes are naturally active at this level, notably among oppressed nations against the domination of core nations. And the UN is indeed an intergovernmental *organization*. It is part of the world-state, but it is part of what Marx called the "abolition" of the state as a system of domination. In this context, the national plurality inherent to the world-system, insofar as it is also a "system of nations," rules out any reasonable prospect of a global state power capable of putting an end to nations. The same goes for any supposedly democratic global project of organizing to "take power" within a supranational political organization that would spell the end of national identities. For these not only include long-term existential and historical experiences, shared wealth, etc.; they also guarantee a pluralist perception of the world, common sense, and common sentiments, which are essential to humanity.

The ideal type of activist interactions, as we know, can be found in NGOs. These are to be understood as a particular type of organization where a "spirit of association" prevails. This spirit contradicts the constantly present pretensions of male-power, capital-power, and competence-power—at least in principle. For in reality, NGOs are most often run by men; or they have an affinity with the "competent"; or they promote adaptation to market constraints (cf. microcredit). But they are also typically the site of struggles for emancipation. At least insofar as the spirit of horizontal cooperation that they profess prevails, they find themselves in affinity with the more or less ephemeral or long-lasting movements and revolts that keep coming in successive waves in a world in constant turmoil. This "rainbow" of concrete affiliations is offered to every person belonging humanity in common. It represents so many sources of perseverance shared with others, loyalty to personal commitments, "distinction" available to all, "points of honor" in the grayness of ordinary life. In the global ecological-political struggle, it is not the "party spirit" that will shine, but the spirit of coalition between disparate and incomparable forms of popular mobilization. The International will be "Global," but it will not follow the party model. It will not be a political organization. It will not be made up of "brother parties," but of sister associations.

## The Age of Uprising

We are engaged not in a "transition," but in a *final struggle*, the challenge of which is to put an end to the ongoing process of *disaster*, if we are to avoid a *catastrophe*, an irreparable fall. This final *struggle*, which those who rule intend to wage as a *war*, responding with violence, only reveals its true nature on a planetary level, where the extent of destruction is given. Struggles from below, wars from above. According to the "dialectic of immanence" between the whole and the parts exposed above, they are carried out on both a local and national scale. It is a civil war, as well as a world war—a "world civil war," in the words of Carl Schmitt. The globality of the *class*-structured world-state is what gives it its "civil" war character. But its "war" dimension comes from the interference between the world-state and the world-system. Such is the ecological war that those who rule wage against humanity and the living. However, due to the resistance it encounters, it has started to take a new course for some time now. And this struggle from below has found a suitable name: "uprising." No ecological "transition" is conceivable without a powerful *uprising*. The age of uprising will last as long as the disaster remains unmitigated. It will last until the specter of catastrophe has been removed. This is the thesis that I would now like to present, through the lens of the analyses proposed throughout this book.

Max Weber distinguished an ideal-typical pair of religious actors, the priest and the prophet, who are at once inseparable and discordant. The priest is in charge of the institution. The prophet makes it tremble, while at the same time sublimating it; he commits himself to the uncertain crests of the received faith. In analogous terms—and only analogous—we are today led to relate the "activist" and the "militant" to each other. The logic according to which each of these figures operates is not the same, even if there are militant-activists. "Activism" concerns political parties, movements, or associations, whose members are durably committed to long-term social transformations. "Militancy" concerns a particular concrete cause, interpreted as being of universal interest. Its reference points, the critical cultures that give rise to it, invite militants to forge ahead off the paths of everyday life, at their own risk and peril, pushing the initiative beyond civil disobedience to the confines of infringement of the legal order, denounced from above as "violence."

Official discourse likes to reduce militancy to "avant-gardism," given the fact that militants do not hesitate to offend property laws when they deem them illegitimate, nor to defy the prohibitions of public liberties. In reality, the two approaches are quite different. "Avant-gardists," let us call them, whether at the front of demonstrations or on the margins, expressly target "capital." And the role that they intend to play in the collective effort must be recognized as such, even if it is doubtful that the symbolic smashing of shop windows or confrontations with the police will cause the slightest harm. Their approach can be described as "parasitic," in the sense that they graft onto pre-existing movements, intervening only to instruct people in the meaning that the other demonstrators should give to their action. Militancy, by contrast, consists of specific, singular initiatives with concrete social or environmental objectives. It does not attack capital in a general-abstract mode; it reveals the concrete destructive effects of the "abstract" goal of profit. It says "no" to this or that airport or highway, to this or that type of agricultural or industrial production, but it does so in order to put forward concrete alternative solutions.

Militancy has long been present in the realm of environmentalism. Defending forests in India and Brazil, blocking the construction of airports in Japan, or that of pipelines in the United States… In France, the Notre-Dame-des-Landes "zone to defend" (*zone à défendre*, ZAD), in the distant wake of the Fight for the Larzac, was a decisive event. But in many places, it is becoming clear that we are shifting from a time of experiments to a time of systematic environmental confrontation with the complex of modern dominations. The French movement Earth Uprisings (*Les Soulèvements de la Terre*), which appeared in 2021 in the spirit of the global climate movement that dates back several decades, is significant in this regard. They have chosen a "name" that is particularly apt to signify the concept they are implementing. I will therefore use it as a *common* noun, to designate a phenomenon that has appeared in various parts of the world and is potentially universal. These "earth uprisings" invite humans to reclaim their common wealth, to assume their responsibility for sustaining life, and to band together in significant local projects. They call on each and every one of us to find our place, our niche, in this collective human enterprise. They are concretely committed to the universal in the long term, in the long duration of the disaster to be overcome. There is indeed some reason to believe that "an uprising cannot be dissolved." This is what I would like to articulate through four concepts: the national-global network, the new alliance, the modernocene, and inhabitation.

First, let's consider the relationship between uprisings and organizations on a national and global scale. Uprisings takes the form of networks. As could be seen in the example of the Yellow Vests Movement (*Mouvement des gilets jaunes*), they concern the appropriation of a territory, of which the vital substance is being destroyed by the dominant class's race for profit or "vain glory." They manifest themselves in the art of crafting a coordinated list of sites for initiatives across an entire country, a sign of "national" political maturity. But, for this reason, they are just as much in affinity with activist, associative, or union activities, which are "national" as well, and which different fractions of the popular class develop on the basis of gender or work relations. In this sense, uprisings establish themselves on the terrain of "politics," but they offer political action a new task that must be identified.

The novelty of uprisings is not in their environmental activism, but in their material structuring on a national level and their global aims. Uprisings affect a wide range of sectors, from agriculture, mining, and manufacturing to transportation, communications, urban planning, and public health. They do not follow the same rhythm as parties, which have an agenda to which they must necessarily adjust their plans and mobilizations. The agenda of uprisings is determined by scandalous occurrences of ecocide, which come to light piecemeal, but more and more quickly with the sharpening of people's critical scrutiny. Networks, as the form of uprisings, cannot replace political organizations, which are responsible for conceiving overall programs. But uprisings conspire with parties since they focus on the same social-ecological totality. This is why the organizations that declare their support for them act neither as guarantors nor as a means of recuperation. Between networks and organizations, there is an inevitable game of mirrors that calls for a critical cross-examination of perspectives.

To return to the concept of the "modern nation-state" developed in the preceding chapter, uprisings top off a people's intention to appropriate in common a territory defined as "*all* of ours," against the grip—the "taking" (*nehmen*), which according to Carl Schmitt establishes the law (*nomos*)—of the dominant class. But they do not pretend that this territory is "ours *alone*." On the contrary, in the spirit of a social struggle on a global scale, they call for the collective control of all human activity on the planet. Indeed, they feed an internationally contagious fever, sustained by the similarity of the modern ruling class's aggressions throughout the world. Each uprising spreads ideas across borders to others. And this is how all of us are "interpellated," invited to assume our vocation as citizens of the world, our responsibility to sustain life.

Secondly, uprisings are what verify the *upheaval* (analyzed above) that appears within the triangular duel on a global scale, in an age of ultimodernity. I've approached this phenomenon from the standpoint of its summits, particularly with reference to bodies like the IPCC, where the general outlines of a new alliance between "competence" and common people are emerging. But cooperation at the grassroots, with immediate mutual support in a concrete struggle, is something entirely different from convergence at the top. Especially since it is not just the people from below who are seeking the support of an elite. Today, it is the officially accredited experts in hard science, especially earth science, who are coming, dismayed, to cooperate, to mix their knowledge and their know-how with that of the common people. Scientists, whistleblowers, and clinical patients; naturalists, hydrologists, geologists, agronomists, doctors, veterinarians, meteorologists, chemists and physicists, architects and urban planners—there is something for everyone. There are also many who refuse to take the place reserved for them in large productivist corporations, inviting their peers to do the same and to move from a right-wing alliance with capital to a left-wing alliance with the fundamental class—with the ulterior motive, of course, of leading the movement. But in uprisings, common people learn once more that alliances also mean struggles.

A fantasy haunts the daydreams of some on the left. Some people wonder what the new social force will be that will come to take over from the industrial "working class" in its role as the "motor" of history and popular emancipation. A new middle class? An urban class? A management class? An intellectual class? This is not, in my opinion, the right way to envisage the future. This is not how the "history" of twentieth-century popular struggles unfolded. For better or worse, it has always been a matter of building alliances between the common people—workers/employees/peasants, depending on the case—and decisive strata of the competent, establishing a balance of power capable of rolling back capital. It is therefore useless to speculate on a mythical "class-in-itself-and-for-itself" as the predestined bearer of the universality to come. As the class structure of modern society, in its specifically "metastructural" form analyzed throughout this book, has not changed, let us instead question this shaky process that can only occur in the great equilibria of the "triangular duel." And we can agree that this "new alliance" is most clearly outlined in "uprisings."

Thirdly, we must return to the Marxian project of abolishing "capital and private property." As we have seen, the weakness of this project lay in the fact that its counterpart was a tacit blend of discursive communist cooperation and hierarchical socialist organization. This mix was at the heart of historical Marxism. Philology has been inviting us, for some time, to notice that, in his late writings, Marx warned against the power of the competent (cf. *Critique of the Gotha*

*Program*), and was particularly interested in cooperative, communist land management (cf. his letters to Vera Zassoulitch). This is the conceptual premise that justifies my own work, which is to take up Marx's theory from the top. But the Marxism that really existed, in affinity with the historical moment, was the one found in *Capital*: industrial Marxism.

Yet, the same ambiguity is reproduced when, in the opposite critical approach, we come to replace "Anthropocene" with "Capitalocene." Capital-power is certainly the great destroyer. But the two modern factors of social class, capital and competence, work together, as we have seen, in the production of ecological disaster. The right concept is the one that questions this structural couple that is associated with modern nation relations and gender relations. The appropriate term to designate it is therefore not "Capitalocene," but "Modernocene," a barbaric term for a modern reality that associates class relations with nation relations and gender relations. It reveals all its truth in the time we live in, which is not postmodernity, nor the beginning of eternity, but ultimodernity, the ultimate scale of modernity, to be confronted as such, at the intersection of the abstraction of abstract wealth through capitalist profit-making, which prevails in markets, and the abstraction of vain glory through competence, which prevails in organizations. In this ultimodernity, humans *"interpellate" each other*, for interpellation belongs eminently to the metastructural essence of modernity, to its perpetual new beginning. In the midst of disaster, history continues, constantly coming back to life, through thousands of discourses and thousands of dreams.

Finally, uprisings point to an ultimate challenge: to humanely inhabit the world among the living.[6]

We find the illustration of this in the fable that is told, here and there, in the form of a surprising practice. What does it mean to endow a river, a valley, or a mountain with legal personality? Such a claim seems meaningless. For the law only exists if it is capable of defending itself, or at least of trying. By assigning rights to a river, we simply declare that we pledge ourselves to defend it as a living organism and provider of life; that it is not foreign to us; and that our lives depend on its own—even more so the lives of the communities it connects. Aren't river networks branch-shaped, much like arteries? Rivers are most often internal to nation-states because they were the vehicles for the complex of exchanges and organizations that allowed them to emerge and flourish—which is also true when they mark their borders. Their arteries are also ours. If the human condition is only really expressed in fables, it's because it is contradictory. In reality, we, humans, are alone in the world when faced with the tasks of life. Of course, we can certainly mobilize other forces to repair or preserve what remains. But only we can do this. As we alone have the power to destroy, we alone have the power to hinder destruction. Only we can understand our reasons for doing so. But the perils that assail us and the means that are at our disposal concern all living people. For what is at stake is the habitability of the earth, which serves as a common habitat for animals and plants. Our sensitive connection with living beings and their ecosystems produces multiple reminders. The droughts due to our excessive carbon emissions, the pestification of the soil, and the plasticization of the seas, all of which affects life cycles, remind us of the common destiny shared between humans and other living beings, including plants. The uninhabitability of the earth is affecting big cats, encircled by highways, at the same time as humans who sleep on the sidewalks of the great urban "arteries."

At a time when humans are eating so poorly, suffering from hunger or being force-fed, and watching mother earth wither away, the industrial worker, once the quintessential worker, has given way to the farmer, prey to ethnocide and yet the last resort. As victims of land grabbing, subject to perpetual debt, and direct witnesses of water stress, soil erosion, and the decline of biodiversity, farmers—at least those who belong to the common people—find themselves forced to adopt practices of preservation and cooperation that point the way forward for the human community as a whole. It is therefore hardly surprising that ecological resistance is often organized around their struggles.

If the fight is difficult, it is because these infantrymen must resist the artillery of the opposing camp. But this is the common task of the great army of common people, an army that engages in struggles rather than wars. Acts of "sabotage" entrusted to special commandos are not enough. They only make sense as part of a general effort to disarm the ecocidal powers of those above. The concept of "disarming" is quite appropriate. Disarm the highway, aeronautical, and maritime conglomerates. Disarm advertising—the commercial dictatorship over our needs. Disarm even the ingenuously criminal weather report, which every day celebrates the happiness of sunshine and deplores the sadness of rain. Disarm the dominations of production and the dominations of consumption. The dominations of genderism, virilism, and ablism. The dominations of nations. The work of peace requires a relentless struggle for disarmament. It seeks its way, against those who maintain their grip from above, in embrace and release, in poetic surprise.

Let us return now to the question posed in the title of this book: Can common people govern? It must be clear that such governance—or in classical terms, such a "government"—can only be conceived as a hegemonic alliance with a left-wing elite, because common people can only push back against capital-power in symbiosis with a fraction of competence-power. This alliance is only possible through the triple practice of participating in organizations, associations, and uprisings, from the local level to the global level. If it is true, according to the hypothesis that guides this book, that any attack on the ecological order stems from a social relation of domination, the logic of emancipation is at one with ecological logic. And vice versa. But the ecological struggle is nothing if it is not global. It is therefore what brings the human community together, not just in ecological terms, but also, inseparably, in terms of emancipation. It brings us together as a world-nation turned against the dominations of the world-state (with its class and gender structures) and the unequal world-system. It is in the world-nation that common people realize their political and ecological potential. It is no longer a question of "mastering" the natural order, but of protecting it. Powerful affects, which call for a new "treatise on the passions," come to support us. The ardent, insurgent pleasure of making the dominant class retreat under our blows, mixed with the happiness of a gardener who sees nature survive the blows that the dominant class has dealt to it—this is what Spinoza would have called "beatitude." Yet, this is in danger of vanishing at any moment. Revolutions that fail are postponed until later. "Good times will come again." But this is not how our ecological history works, for the revolution cannot wait. It's now or never. Between disaster, which is accelerating, and catastrophe, which is terminal, we live in the haste of the final days.

## Notes

1 On the concept of interpellation, see Jacques Bidet, "The Interpellated Subject: Beyond Althusser and Butler," *Crisis & Critique* 2, no. 2 (2017).

2 Jacques Bidet, *A Political Ecology of Common People*, trans. David Broder (New York: Routledge, 2024).

3 Giovanni Arrighi, taking up an old idea of Marx, put forward the theme of a cyclicality of world hegemony, the power of core countries being founded successively on industry, then on commerce, and finally on finance, before letting others play the role of hegemon. But cyclical reproduction does not in itself constitute a historical trend. See Giovanni Arrighi, *Adam Smith in Beijing: Lineages of the Twenty-First Century* (London: Verso, 2007).

4 Althusser puts forward a pertinent critique of the "structural totality" conceived, according to a Hegelian conception, as immanent to its parts. Here we are dealing with a completely different issue: the dynamic relations between national structuration and world structuration.

5 In the case of Ukraine, for example, common people's logic is faced with a tangle of imperialisms. US imperialism, the major form, dominates not only through the thousands of military bases the it has throughout the world, but also through its financial and monetary power, which ensures its stranglehold over most of the globe, not to mention the Big Tech networks—the key to communications pre-eminence—that tightly surround all continents. But the people of Europe must also confront the regional imperialism of the Russian Empire, so dangerously violent in the convulsions of its agony, by assuming responsibility towards neighboring nations that form a historically disputed periphery between the East and the West. As for the people of France, they will not forget that their primary responsibility is to fight against their own imperialism in this context.

6 See Paul Guillibert, *Terre et capital: pour un communisme du vivant* [The Earth and Capital: For a Communism of the Living] (Paris: Éditions Amsterdam, 2021); and Stéphane Haber, *Critique de l'antinaturalisme: études sur Foucault, Butler, Habermas* [The Critique of Antinaturalism: On Foucault, Butler, and Habermas] (Paris: PUF, 2006).

## References

Arrighi, Giovanni. *Adam Smith in Beijing: Lineages of the Twenty-First Century*. London: Verso, 2007.

Bidet, Jacques. "The Interpellated Subject: Beyond Althusser and Butler." *Crisis & Critique* 2, no. 2 (2017): 62–85.

———. *A Political Ecology of Common People*. Translated by David Broder. New York: Routledge, 2024.

Guillibert, Paul. *Terre et capital: pour un communisme du vivant*. [The Earth and Capital: For a Communism of the Living.] Paris: Éditions Amsterdam, 2021.

Haber, Stéphane. *Critique de l'antinaturalisme: études sur Foucault, Butler, Habermas*. [The Critique of Antinaturalism: On Foucault, Butler, and Habermas.] Paris: PUF, 2006.

# Appendix

## On the Popular Left in France Today

In this appendix to the preceding theoretical essay, I take on a singular object, "France" today. Neither the "literary genre," nor the "narrator," nor the types of questions are the same. It is not about finding a political project such as one that a party can and must propose, nor a socioeconomic program produced by a body of experts. These essential questions are always assumed to be present. But this essay is simply an analysis of the sociopolitical forces at work here and now, and their potential for conflict, alliance, domination, and emancipation. It aims to shed light on the "formal" question of political organization, *die Organizationsfrage*. This question, which opposed Lenin, Kautsky, and Rosa Luxembourg, has continuously preoccupied and troubled the supporters of "rupture." We find this debate today in the opposition between "parties" and "movements." This is the formal dimension, so to say, of popular politics; but, as one might suspect, form has a lot to do with substance.

### A Brief Retrospective of 2012–2022 and Beyond

#### *Expanded Opportunities and Emerging Dangers*

For common people, the "here and now" to be considered—along with that of the planet—is certainly that of the nation-state, where the first contours of the political community take shape. Indeed, this is the space-time in which they most immediately confront the ruling class. This confrontation does not only concern the control and transformation of the state apparatus, supposedly to "abolish" it as an apparatus of domination; it also concerns, correlatively, the control and transformation of that which makes up the material and spiritual substance of the class struggle, a treasure trove of concrete wealth reworked over the centuries: the "nation." As for the "now," when a decisive national political victory is at stake, we must reason in terms of legislature, more precisely in terms of both presidential and legislative periods—since legislative elections, today, in the highly presidential Constitution of France, only serve to confirm presidential elections, being organized almost immediately after them. The paradoxical unity of the Hollande-Macron presidential decade is relevant, insofar as it saw the development of a continuous, unprecedented thrust toward neoliberalism—Sarkozy dreamt it, Hollande and Macron achieved it—to which new forms of resistance and initiative responded.

Presenting a general overview of the "state of politics" in French society today goes beyond the scope of this essay. Readers may consult the programs of various political, associative, and trade-union organizations whose aim is to transform the political situation in France.[1] My only propose here is to contribute to their reflections by examining, in the light of the concepts put forward throughout this book, the revolutionary potential that common people still have despite the setbacks that have been inflicted upon them. What, then, can we learn from this decade, which saw the emergence of a new generation of political actors and actresses who are now taking part in politics? Within the limits of this essay, I will confine myself to discussing a few symptoms that seem significant to me for the future.

*Strikes against the El Khomri law (Loi travail), 2016–2017.* "Popular power"—i.e., common people's hold, limited and by no means perennial, but incontestable, over the course of national life—has had to face a long series of attacks: a reform of the French Labor Code that makes employment more fragile and uncertain; an increase of the statutory retirement age; commitment to the privatization of railways; and multiple attacks on the health system, the school and university systems, public freedoms, etc. The neoliberal "powers that be" have succeeded in inflicting—despite fierce resistance and strike movements, certainly not as massive as those of May 1968, but longer in some sectors—a sequence of heavy defeats. "Workers' strongholds," formerly ardent centers of trade unionism, had already been weakened for decades by successive waves of offshoring and de-mergers, making business structures increasingly diverse and precarious. Workers have been unable to withstand this head-on impact.

However, this is not the whole story. The national strike movements against these attacks reminded us of the fact that the modern nation is built like a business, made up of cogs of all kinds, each of which is essential to the functioning of the whole. As we know, large companies themselves are hotbeds of class struggle. This observation already fueled the old "general strike" schemes of the previous century. To block the production process, one sector was clearly essential in this respect: transportation (of people, goods, and energy). In May 1968, it was the automotive industry, a central and highly symbolic link in the chain, that triggered the strike movement. Capitalists' response was to dismantle large industrial companies. But this did not lead to the demise of the nation-state, which has been the terrain of the struggles of the past ten years. These struggles were fierce because the strike movements affected the entire population, both as factors of disturbance in daily life and as calls to join the movement. At times, popular commitment was so strong that it could have led to victory. And yet, in the end, the momentum was broken.

*Nuit debout ("Rise up at night"), 2016–2017.* With the general strike (*grève générale*) in check, all that remained was the "general dream" (*rêve général*). This dream, however, was something substantial. For it was a dream not only of "overthrowing the regime," but also of establishing an *alternative way of living together*. Impalpable material, but explosive. The "Nuit debout" movement and the "occupations" of public squares, which had begun before the strike, secretly conspired to build commitments on the ground. The various social strata and fractions are not spontaneously in unison. Popular struggles take place in discordant times and places, on several stages at once, where the same languages are not necessarily spoken. Translation, however, is bound to be possible, because, faced with a common enemy, these struggles "*interpellate*" each other, even if obliquely. Links were established between the labor movement and the Nuit debout movement. The leader of the CGT spoke to the people occupying the Place de la République, his time being limited to three minutes, just like the dozens of other speakers, according to the rule established that night. It was becoming clear that the capitalist order would not yield without the irruption of the "working class" in direct contact with the material apparatus of production. The failure was also an accumulation of experiences on both sides.

*The Yellow Vests Movement, 2018–2020.* The Yellow Vests Movement (*mouvement des Gilets jaunes*) was clearly a result of the urban/rural divide. The explosion of urbanization, which is constantly accelerating, has transformed demographics. The attraction of the city is a universal phenomenon. It manifests itself in the massive migrations to the marginalized neighborhoods and slums of the major cities of the South. Megacities tend to suck in and *absorb* vital forces, just as core countries do for the peripheries. *Major* cities are where most jobs; education, training, and health institutions; social services; shops, etc., are now located, along with the densest networks of cultural relations and activities, the best internet access, and so on. They are also where the major transport hubs are located.

If "property" is nothing other than the *socially recognized* use of something, the appropriation of space, as a place of life and opportunity, employment, production, training, care, etc., is not an *add-on* to class relations. It is a substantial dimension of it. This is how the labor movement exerted a diffuse influence over large businesses by limiting the *ownership* of capital, and thus the power of the capitalists, who could certainly use their means of production to make profits, but under specific conditions concerning workers' compensation, hardships, job security, recognized qualifications, etc., all of which define class relations according to the balance of political and economic power. This is what neoliberalism has sabotaged. Similarly, the decline of small towns, which were once economic, administrative, cultural, and political hubs (in Europe at least), is analogous to the "destruction" of large businesses under the blows of neoliberalism. What has thus disappeared are spaces that people had, in an age-old class confrontation, somewhat appropriated, in such a way that they were punctuated by public services, in a context where local employment was still available, all of this together constituting a fabric of social awareness and possible democratic consultation. The explosion of May 1968 was echoed and relayed right down to even the smallest businesses of France's heartland.

This world is now something of the past. And it is in this context that the Yellow Vests created a surprise. They were able to implement an unprecedented form of practice. Blocking roundabouts played a role similar to that of occupying workplaces. In reality, this is more than just an analogy, since the daily commute to and from work is an essential part of the production process. It was also a symbolic infringement on the domination of one class over France. Online coordination enabled spatially distant groups to make decisions at the grassroots level, similar to workshop-by-workshop walkouts.

An entire population, which was assumed to be more or less out of the game, manifested unsuspected political awareness, knowledge, and know-how, with the use of cell phones being combined with friendly face-to-face meetings. This population showed itself capable of carrying out long-term "horizontal" action on a national scale, fermenting a sustained social insubordination that gradually expanded to all circles of poor people who felt expropriated, and even to wider circles of people who felt their future was increasingly uncertain. This is what the "Yellow Vests," despite the repression against them, revolted against, inviting the "general dream" as a motor for action, and inspiring a spirit of resistance that has not wavered since.

*The Citizens' Climate Convention, 2019–2020.* This episode was a direct result of the Yellow Vests Movement. As the conclusion to the so-called Great National Debate (*Grand Débat National*) to which the movement had given rise, it provides an interesting object for reflection. Constituted by drawing lots based on a sociological breakdown of French society, notably by age, sex, and socioeconomic background, its make-up differed from that of any other elected assembly. The ruling class was reduced to its modest size relative to the population. Amazingly, its proposals very much reflected left-wing social and environmental ambitions. It will come as no surprise that, for this reason, the Macron government has made minimal use of it. Nevertheless, due to circumstances, this was a historical precedent that will be difficult to exorcise completely. It illustrates the fact that common people have left-wing ideas, even when they mostly vote for right-wing candidates. In the moment of reflection and perspective that pollsters' questions provoke, the aspirations to bring about a future of emancipation and environmental protection are expressed. In the organized hullabaloo of electoral festivities, those who voice the dominant discourse, carried by a staff of notables familiar to voters, popularized by the colluding media and the supposedly "competent," regain the upper hand. It remains to seen what lessons can be drawn from this unique phenomenon for a popular project of political organization.

*The time of the pandemic, 2020–2021.* The pandemic, in its national dimension, provided the neoliberal powers that be with an exceptional margin for action. Only the environmental movement, because of its modes of action, and perhaps also because it is now based on widely shared evidence, in principle at least, was able to impose itself from time to time in the media (cf. Extinction Rebellion).

Labor unions, by contrast, had their hands tied. They were prevented from any form of public expression in the streets and workplaces, while privatizations continued to push forward in the tranquil silence of the mountaintops. Women's struggles were obscured by the very exaltation of the heroism of the front-line nurses; the others were just expected to behave themselves, and nothing could be said or shown of the faceless crowds that, early every morning, shared the major risk of taking the bus or the train. Only marginally could any tensions between the institutions of "competence"-power be observed. Competence was particularly represented in the Conseil scientifique COVID-19, an ad hoc body that President Macron set up as a veritable "War Council" to discreetly adjust the observations of specialists to the requirements of his political agenda. The media coverage, under discreet neoliberal influence, left little room for a "left-wing alliance" to take shape. The unions were certainly on the frontlines, but they found themselves ill-equipped to face this unprecedented type of responsibility—not the least because of the blows dealt to occupational health care and the "Health and Safety Councils," which had been under union control in all large companies since 1968, and which were denied any competence whatsoever. The medical luminaries, legitimized by their high positions in hospitals, feared they would be delegitimized if they entered the political arena, by speaking out—openly—about what they knew only too well about the incompetence of successive governments. In the context of a weakened popular left, there was no alliance between the common people and the "competent." This stood in contrast with 1968 and the decade that followed. Thus, the pandemic left the popular forces relatively on the sidelines for some time.

*The 2023 French pension reform strikes.* This was undoubtedly the most powerful movement of past ten years. Its aim was to oppose the increase of the retirement age from 62 to 64. What made it remarkable was that it brought together all the major unions, from the most reformist (UNSA, CFDT, FO) to the most revolutionary (CGT and Solidaires). The vast majority of the population and all left-wing parties supported it. It kept France on its toes, just as the 2016–2017 movement had done previously. And, for a while, it looked like it would win. It never wavered. Eventually, the government's bill won out by a just a few votes, demonstrating the extent to which the French Parliament is hardly representative of the socio-professional reality of the country. Despite everything, it was a great experience that schooled a new generation of political actors and actresses in popular political practice.

### *The Rainbow on an Uncertain Horizon*

If we look back now over the past ten years, we see a number of new features emerging. The rainbow, an emblem of gender struggles and used by LGBTQ movements, now seems to be just as suitable for bringing together all struggles for emancipation.[2] See the "freedom marches" in fall 2020. The important battles won during this decade often brought together a whole range of "colors": for example, the abandonment of the airport project in Notre-Dame-des-Landes, the Europacity project in the Gonesse Triangle, and the "1000-cow farm" project in Picardy. These may only be micro-victories, but they renewed the collective imagination. These experiences of fusion at the grassroots between social and environmental demands were bathed in the same *democratic* climate as the toughest union struggles. It thus became clear that, if not the outbreak, at least the *continuation* of the strikes against labor and transport reforms was never the result of supposedly overarching union or political power, but of local and sectoral "potential for action," which snowballed through a process of reciprocal recognition, and only existed insofar as the initiatives were reinitialized on a daily basis. This grassroots impetus, the hallmark of a collective political consciousness, could be found just as much within the labor unions, the associations, and the scattered Yellow Vests Movement. Thus new pathways are now crossing. The rise of popular environmental awareness is changing the balance of power in favor of what is common and long-term, and this is clearly the case for the railway network, which calls for centralized, multi-decade planning (while surprisingly revealing itself as a possible field for cooperative enterprises). Neoliberal power is thus expected to address a new issue, on which the left seems to have more to say than the right: environmental *planning*. An issue with a great future ahead of it.

In recent years, feminist struggles have been particularly focused on male violence, to the point of imposing the concept of "feminicide," a milestone in the history of social criticism. It is true that, as a backlash, the relationship between gender and class domination (as well as "race" and class domination) seems to have faded into the background, to the detriment of the latter. But a new impetus was given by a #MeToo movement *à la française*, a movement of "women all together" that, beyond the heroism of those who dared to take part, demonstrated the groundswell carrying them forward. This display of what may be considered male turpitude in a position of power, while giving impetus to gender struggles as a whole, has an equally powerful impact on the class struggles that overdetermine them. It casts suspicion on all social hierarchies, revealing their relationship to sex and the use of the body. Exposing the male god for what he is, exhibiting the misery of his sex when he makes it the instrument of his hierarchical arbitrariness, the #MeToo movement jointly reveals and denounces the class, gender, and "racial" positions that allow him to pounce on his prey, which the "triptych of domination" offers to his appetites. This is the eminent truth of "wokism," this call to awakening that comes to us today from the social sciences, and which the reaction, led by the Minister of National Education, has tried to turn into a strawman.

Compared to the tasks that the common people could set themselves in the last century against dominations within the nation-state, a popular victory over the global hydra of neoliberalism has become more difficult to conceive. As the old revolutionary project moved further and further away from the horizon, an *individualist* reversal of representations and affects took place among the common people, expressed politically not so much in the form of electoral abstention, which is often a political stance, but rather in a withdrawal from "politics," for lack of space. This is also the space that we must confront today. For, it is not an empty space: A new front line has emerged on the far right, which is making steady progress, confirming the Right's stranglehold on French and European society. The spectacular rise in the number of seats won by the Rassemblement National (RN, National Rally) during the last legislative elections is the expression of this far-right party's growing influence over a large part of the country, over people who are neither the "poorest," nor the most marginalized, nor the most subject to precariousness, but who, although often employed, salaried or self-employed, find themselves poorly endowed in terms of income, qualifications, social services, and perspectives for the future.

This concerns a large portion of the "common people." It is particularly the case in territories where powerful trade-union and political movements once flourished, notably in large companies that have now vanished. The next generation has lost all memory of these, and social solidarity has been replaced by state-run social assistance, which affects a large fringe of what I call "people B." Those who escape this miserable condition are inclined to imagine that salvation can only come from the determination of each individual to find a job rather than relying on public welfare programs, i.e., on other people's labor. This philosophy, which is the RN's, has steadily gained ground. We saw its electoral consequences in 2022: The left, even if it had reconstituted itself, made no progress in terms of the number of voters, i.e., in public opinion in general, while the far right broke all its previous records. Clearly, this unprecedented situation is now at the center of the "question of organization."

### *How Should Popular Political Action Be Organized?*

During this ten-year period, according to my analysis of modern society and the present time, and with regard to the points that I consider decisive for a popular political practice (uniting people A and people B, groundedness, the symbiosis of heterogeneous politicalities, "competent danger"), I put forward a precisely defined strategy for political organization.[3] In an article published in *Libération*,[4] I summarily formulated a project proposed at the time as an alternative to both the "party model" and the "movement model": the "collective model." Today, I would prefer to say the "cooperative model," in view of the plurality that it aims to integrate, far from the fusionist spirit attached to the word "collective." This project made sense in the context of the political perspective that had opened at that time: that of a new dynamic of popular unity, making a positive left-wing alliance conceivable. It remains to be seen, of course, whether this perspective will remain relevant in the context that began to take shape in 2022.

The terms of this project were the following:

> May the various organizations of the popular left, without abandoning their own identity or dynamics, call for the constitution, in each locality or constituency, of collectives that unite all people who, as members or not of a party, a union, or an association, are ready to commit themselves to the same common orientations. And may they grant these local collectives, in which they themselves will be present and influential through their members, full political responsibility at their own level: the tasks of leading the social and civic struggles, of proposing candidates for local and national elections, etc. Not mere "general assemblies," which are

> often useful but inherently volatile, but lasting and incontestable collectives through their democratic form of association. The disciplined rise through the ranks is not very difficult to conceive, since what is essential is that the central collective is drawn from the ranks of the grassroots collectives and remains under their control, thus being all the more capable of imagination, initiative, and reaction.
>
> The different parties and movements, present and future, will find there their natural place there, where they will develop according to their own cultures, to be shared between the various organizations of the popular left as a common good. But power will remain anchored at the bottom. This, of course, will require some correlative principles of organization that are quite simply democratic. First and foremost, there must be a limit to the number of terms that leaders and candidates for elective office can serve, since by the end of their term they will have amassed a capital of power that must be returned to the people.
>
> This is the only way for a large, diverse, and coherent popular political force to emerge in France today. And perhaps "the people," composed of workers and employees, of the unemployed and self-employed, a large number of whom the Yellow Vests are the image and symbol, and who turn out to be so "politicized," will able to recognize this force as their own. [5]

What can be said about such a project? It is certainly a utopia, with so many obstacles standing in the way of its implementation within the social forces concerned, particularly among the competent. But its aim was to point the way forward. It did not propose to do away with parties or movements, but to include them in a common organization as "caucuses," so to say, i.e., laboratories of ideas, experiences, and initiatives, capable of allowing strategic proposals to mature through discordant discussions. They would form the hard cores, the places of memory and reflection where those who feel ready to engage further in the political battle would come together and train, each "fraction," as it used to be said, fighting for the triumph of its own line. At the same time, they would find in this common and diverse space a climate conducive to their renewal. The aim was not to amalgamate them, to cast them in the same mold, but to get them to meet and cooperate at the base rather than at the summit—collaboration, in action and reflection, between citizens and not just leaders. This would also allow people active in political parties, unions, and associations to discover and recognize each other (thus forging a lasting link to feminist, environmental, anti-racist, pacifist, and multicultural struggles), as well as those ready to commit themselves on an ad hoc basis to these local collectives. Thus, the diverse cultures of political parties and associations would intersect, from those who choose to make a lifelong commitment (or so they think in any case) to those who intend to "do something" in a defined situation, for a particular cause they are convinced is essential to the common cause.

This scheme combines creative disorder at the grassroots, drawing on the experience and imagination of common people and their capacity for initiative, with collective rigor at the top, where all vectors of the fundamental class must converge, based on jointly conducted socioeconomic and geopolitical analyses. These grassroots collectives (or cooperatives) would derive their political effectiveness—the credibility allowing them to assert themselves in battle—from their indisputable democratic form. In France, for example, this could take the form of a genuine "association" as defined by law, with officials regularly elected for a defined period. Membership would be clearly national but under the responsibility of the local collectives, to which everyone would make their contribution. This is, of course, an ideal type that should be materialized in local entities of a sufficiently modest size so that common people can feel at home and actively intervene on a day-to-day basis, but capable of regrouping into larger coherent entities when the time comes to choose, for example, candidates for national office or to distribute roles among city council members.

The ship, thus ballasted at the bottom of the hold, would undoubtedly be more capable of weathering the storm, of slipping between the reefs, of changing course when necessary, and of boarding at the decisive moment, than some large political raft tied from the top. It would be essential for this form of organization to be established not around a short-term electoral program, put forward for the duration of a legislative term, embodied in a providential, presidential figure; but around a long-term worldview, around values, objectives, and strategic convictions that a large number of people feel capable of sustainably committing their existence to—this *long*-term standpoint also being the condition and the guarantee of a *broader* horizon, where national concerns become part of a global perspective, in the worldwide struggle for human emancipation and the protection of life.

This was the utopian but indicative perspective that I was led to put forward at a specific historical moment, that of the decade spanning from 2012 to 2022. And the analysis must clearly be reconsidered today, which is what I will attempt to do at the end of this appendix.

## The Rise of La France Insoumise and the Political Situation in 2024

The French presidential and legislative elections of 2022 undoubtedly marked a turning point in the trajectory of the popular left, as they resulted in the constitution of the Nouvelle Union populaire écologique et sociale (NUPES, New Ecological and Social People's Union). But the event within the event seems to be the pre-eminence secured by La France Insoumise (LFI, France Unbowed). This is therefore the starting point for the rest of the story, if we are to take it any further.

### *The Paradoxes of La France Insoumise*

Manuel Cervera-Marzal has undoubtedly conducted the most in-depth study of La France Insoumise.[6] It is worth noting that he approaches it from the angle of "populism." This is certainly justified. It is understandable, however, that I am interested in this concept insofar as it opposes "movements" against "parties."

"Populism," broadly defined as a political model that directly unites a population with a leader, finds particularly favorable conditions for its recurrent appearance in France. For, in contrast to its European neighbors, the Constitution of the Fifth Republic, established by Charles De Gaulle, gives the president of the republic exorbitant power. Every five years, citizens are called upon to choose their leader. This is the high point of the nation's political pulse, a time charged with emotion, during which aspiring presidents take the stage. The resulting potential for populism is likely to manifest itself across the political spectrum. It has long existed on the far right, from Jean-Marie Le Pen's Front National (FN, National Front) to Marine Le Pen's Rassemblement National (RN, National Rally). Today, it can also be found on the neoliberal right, in Emmanuel Macron's so-called centrism. But also on the popular left, within La France Insoumise, under the leadership of Jean-Luc Mélenchon. These three cases are obviously very different. In the first case, the party model is crushed by a quasi-dynastic power capable of imposing itself across an entire network by relying on a discourse that supposedly intersects the defense of popular interests with that of national sovereignty. In the second case, the leader, having succeed in rallying a parliamentary majority committed to his neoliberal outlook, and in orienting the legislative and executive powers at his disposal in this direction, is able to implement his policies without having to abide by the conditions set by the various parties that contributed to his election. He has no need to crush party power: He can simply ride roughshod over it. The results of the 2022 legislative elections, which put an end to the absolute majority that the great leader had enjoyed, will certainly make his task more difficult. But he still has some room to maneuver, for the new right that he embodies (despite its modernist cultural veneer) has essentially integrated the social requirements of the old right, wrongly referred to as "the right." In the third case, the leader must strive to extinguish the "party spirit" that remains alive within the social or green left, whose values and collective memory he must integrate and manage on his own behalf, while rejecting its internal, deliberative, and elective practices.

"Populism" does not prevent the far right from being what it is: reactionary and sometimes a bit fascist. Nor the right from being ruthlessly right-wing. Nor La France Insoumise from being part of a popular left lineage, heir to, among other things, Marxist traditions, with reference to class struggles, imperialism, etc., while integrating the feminist and environmental demands that have since risen to the horizon of the left as a whole. There are therefore profound differences between these various "populisms," which oppose each other on the type of society and values to be brought about. In all three cases, however, we find the figure of the leader and his or her immediate relationship with "the people."

The specificity of La France Insoumise is that it is a *movement* that aims to wipe out and establish its hegemony over the pre-existing left-wing organizations based on the *party* model. There is a surprising contradiction here. On the one hand, a radically democratic, anti-capitalist, anti-neoliberal *program*, which asserts itself in multiple ways, including on the environmental front. On the other hand, a consciously vindicated *practice*: that of a "movement-under-the-aegis-of-the-leader," which aims to give impetus to such a program. This is at least what I would like to consider by analyzing the latest electoral episode, the 2022 elections, by showing how this blatant contradiction has paradoxically come to be overcome.

The Paradox of La France Insoumise is that it is an undemocratic organization aiming to establish a radical democracy. Cervera-Marzal documents in the most precise way the undemocratic nature of La France Insoumise. This is has become common knowledge, especially since the internal reform that LFI announced in December 2022, and which I will refrain from discussing until it has manifested its effects. I will therefore stick to La France Insoumise as it has historically been known. Internal caucuses that could give rise to organized groupings within the movement are forbidden, as are territorial structures durably patterned on departments or localities, from which could emerge self-conscious personalities or entities likely to put forward independent themes. There are only "action groups" (groupes d'action), initially called "support groups" (groupes d'appui), which are entirely free to pursue their own initiatives, provided they fall within the framework of the program, L'Avenir en commun,[7] which nevertheless remains subject to clarifications from LFI leadership at any time. There is no membership in the sense of membership to a party, with membership dues and a defined location within an organizational structure, such as a "federation" or "chapter," which together form a territorial network. To integrate the formless body of the movement, all it takes is the click of a mouse, which gives you no particular right to take part in the development of the program or the appointment of leaders. Membership is virtual and can be terminated by leadership just as easily with a click of a mouse. Until recently, the composition of the national leadership body, how it operated, and how people became appointed to it remained unknown to the public (and even to members), apart from the list of personalities who most often appear in the media.

Although LFI's *parliamentary group* meets every Tuesday morning to ensure that its members' positions are consistent, it does not differ significantly from the other groups in this respect, for fairly obvious reasons. The general process of drawing up the *political platform* follows its own logic. All members are asked to formulate detailed, well-supported proposals; these are submitted to the judgment of associations, labor unions, and a group of personalities deemed representative; and a team of national leaders is in charge of writing up a summary of the proposals, of which the feasibility and projected costs are submitted to a panel of competent experts. The finalized project is then submitted to a national congress, half of whose members are chosen by lot, and the other half, by central decisionmakers—and it is easy to guess what their respective weight is. The liturgical and festive conditions of the final act do not really lend themselves to discussion or amendment. This skeletal outline obviously does not do justice to the vast amount of thought, work, and exchanges that go into this process, which is certainly very rich in terms of the quality of the participants and the resulting texts.

Jean-Luc Mélenchon not only acknowledges, but also theorizes this undemocratic march toward democracy. In his eyes, what is most important is to "obstruct pluralism and internal democracy."[8] The leader takes center stage. He is not at the top of a hierarchy, as may be the case in a bureaucratized party. He is at the *center*, the center of concentric circles, according to his own onion metaphor. It seems to me that his relationships with those closest to him can be described as "feudal," in the sense of a mutual but unequal personal commitment, with each person's weight depending on their own political capital. As for the total body in motion, another metaphor, similarly claimed by Jean-Luc Mélenchon, suits it: that of a "gaseous" body, in which each particle, each monad, is freely connected to all the others. This is not anarchism, but rather, I would say, a shared individualism, in tune with the liberal zeitgeist.

If the term "gaseous body" is to be taken positively, it is because it points to the political productivity of this infinitely light structuration. Everyone chooses their own niche, and each "action group," local or thematic, sets itself its own tasks—which, according to Cervera-Marzal, are generally minimal in scope, pragmatic rather than reflexive. All this together, however, helps to sustain a certain critical ferment, which translates into nationwide demonstrations and mass mobilizations during election campaigns. The most remarkable activist breakthrough is that which is achieved through digital actions and action groups, which disseminate on a very large scale both the thoughts of the leader, an incomparable pedagogue, and his program, driving waves of popular education among a fraction of young people, particularly students and the urban youth. In short, the political productivity that this "movement" has demonstrated has profoundly altered the political landscape, as could be seen in the 2022 elections.

The program that Jean-Luc Mélenchon carries, *L'Avenir en commun*, ostentatiously highlights the democratic imperatives that he intends to promote through the institutions to be put in place. This is true from the very first chapter, under headings such as "Abolishing the Presidential Monarchy," "Popular Intervention," "Citizen

Conventions," and "Citizen Revolution." When Mélenchon writes in the introduction, "Here I have summarized the philosophy that drives me as the candidate of the program you are about to read,"[9] we are justified in thinking that the free and equal participation of each and every person in political life, particularly within a political movement that aims to radically transform society, constitutes the first article of his philosophical credo, the presupposition of all the others. If this is indeed the case, as the new social order takes shape, it will inevitably lead to the rejection of all presidentialism and the demand for a citizens' revolution at the very heart of the popular organization that drives it. The paradox is therefore that such an undemocratic organization could put forward such democratic schemes. And the paradox within the paradox is that, despite this contradiction, Jean-Luc Mélenchon's presidential campaign subsequently led, if not to victory, at least to a remarkable number of seats in Parliament, enabling a relatively unified popular left to put obstacles in the way of Emmanuel Macron's undertakings.

### *From a Broader Perspective*

To account for this process, we must take up the historical thread from a little earlier. Jean-Luc Mélenchon did not "found" the Front de Gauche (Left Front), as is often said, nor did he produce its program. Rather, this all stemmed from a political resurgence of the popular left that started in 2005 with the "No" campaign against the new European Treaty, which placed Europe under the neoliberal yoke, causing a real trauma and identity crisis within national consciousness. The painful failure in the 2006–2007 presidential election campaign, which saw the "radical left" groups that had just pledged friendship tear themselves apart, was a litmus test. From then on, the desire for unity took over and continued to gain momentum. The Front de Gauche, formed in 2008–2009 as a partnership between the Communist Party—which still had a significant presence in the public arena through the number of its activists and elected officials, and because of its influence in trade unions—and Jean-Luc Mélenchon's small Parti de Gauche (Left Party), the result of a split from the Socialist Party. In 2012, the Front de Gauche took part in the presidential election under a common platform called *L'Humain d'abord* (People First), which testified to a rebirth of the desire for unity. As Cervera-Marzal observes, this platform was very similar to that of the communists in France, Spain, and Portugal.[10] Jean-Luc Mélenchon, an outstanding speaker both on television and in meetings, a seasoned politician, a man of the party apparatus, a man of culture, the bearer of a universalist and critical worldview, a charismatic tribune, was recognized as the best conceivable spokesman.

No one knows what would have happened in 2017 if the Front de Gauche had continued its momentum in the new context of the decomposition of the Socialist Party, i.e., if Jean-Luc Mélenchon hadn't put an end to this experiment by designating himself as the leader of the left, called upon to oversee the remaking of its strategic program. Nor what would have happened next in 2022, when, five years later, neoliberal domination (at the national, European, and global levels) had become even more overwhelming, and environmental destruction more distressing. Let's leave this aside, however, because ruminating on an alternative future doesn't provide any information. Let us instead consider the circumstances of the "success" of 2022. And, to do so, let's go back even further in time.

The left has long known that it can accomplish nothing if it is not united. As soon as it splits into a popular left and an elite left, it is no longer "the left." Only unity makes it possible to reach the heights of government power, without which nothing decisive can be gained. The split between two Internationals in 1921 broke the earlier momentum, until the first major general crisis of capitalism in the 1930s opened a new unitary perspective. Since 1936, nostalgia has remained, nostalgia for insurrections. In 1946, the French Communists thew their considerable weight behind the implementation of the social and economic reforms planned in the Resistance Program.[11] The dark days of the Cold War put an end to this. In 1956, when the right proved incapable of dealing with thc colonial uprisings, the prospect of left-wing unity was back on the agenda. This was short-lived, however, as it proved impracticable to unite the Communist Party, which supported Algerian independence,[12] and the Socialist Party, which could not resign itself to this, or to working with a partner discredited by its allegiance to the Soviet Union. The movement of 1968, which brought together—with a certain degree of discordance, but that's not what is important—all the components of the left, in all areas, from the workplace to the university, including the major institutions of justice, health, culture, etc., where there is a large "competent" population, led to the rebirth of a desire to unite the left, materialized in the *Programme commun*.[13] And if, five decades later, the memory of this has not been lost, it is because social struggles have never ceased since then, in the configuration of the "triangular duel." These struggles have ensured the tenuous but significant links between generations, despite the profound changes in the political and economic contexts (from the local level to the global level), and the cultural metamorphoses that have accompanied them.

This persistent desire for unity cannot be understood as a cultural fact residing in the supposed revolutionary vocation of a certain "people." It exists only through a chain of major events involving both practical struggles and theory, which invites us to return to this present-past. *L'Avenir en commun*, the 2022 program, represents a body of orientations that go back to the Resistance Program, heir to the uprisings of 1936, implemented through the struggles of 1945–1948, relayed by the *Programme commun* of the left of 1972, itself heir to 1968. As for the programs of 2017 and 2022, they are themselves the fruit of the bitter struggles of this period: long railway strikes, the Yellow Vests Movement, environmental victories like Notre-Dame-des-Landes, #MeToo *à la française*, to name only a few highlights, which, again in discordance, share the manifestation of popular creativity. It seems to me that the parallel between François Mitterrand, who was repugnant to the very idea of a program, and Jean-Luc Mélenchon is unjustified in this regard. Mélenchon was, in a way, a "program-candidate." Let us compare 1972 and 2022, 50 years apart. We know what popular enthusiasm the "Common Program of the Left" aroused, perceived as representative of long-held hopes born of constantly renewed popular struggles, stymied by state power in the hands of capitalism. Its campaign launch was a huge success; but at the time, although there was a program and a candidate, the candidate, despite what he said, kept the program at arm's length.[14] In 2022, the same popular enthusiasm was back. The difference was that this time, the candidate made the program his own; he was its spokesperson, and he continued to identify with it even more so as he made it his own. Enthusiasm for the candidate increasingly merged with reasoned enthusiasm for the program that he so magnificently expounded, with the clarity of a teacher, the passion of a politician, and the touch of a poet that sublimated the moment. The paradox in all this is that as he made the program his own, he himself became, to use his own words, "the candidate of the program," a program-candidate, a program turned candidate. He faded behind the program.

### *The Turning Point of 2022*

Under these conditions, the common program presented in 2022 was, at least in its broad outlines, likely to win the conviction of a united left. Its starting point is "people's problems," including salaries, pensions, employment, housing, health, education, and security. It links them to the political and economic conditions of neoliberalism. It places the ecological peril at the forefront, relating it to neoliberal social disorder. It integrates the new demands of feminism, as expressed more forcefully year after year, through multiple, incessant struggles. It is in line with the horizon of alter-globalization. In short, it is as red as a communist program, as green as a green-party program, as humanist as a socialist program, as "rainbow" colored as feminist, anti-racist, and universalist programs. On all these points, it goes further than previous programs in the multiple details of the diagnosis and remedies for the various ills of our society. It does not just incorporate the proposals put forward by unions and associations; it brings them together in an economically coherent project, meeting the criteria and requirements of certain fractions of competence-power that manifested themselves as stakeholders. Under these conditions, it easy to understand why it was favored by this part of the electorate, which ranges from certain fractions of the Socialist Party and Green Party to the Communist Party and La France Insoumise, whose political horizon is that of a popular left. It is also easy to see why it had a certain power of attraction well beyond these parties.

In short, the desire for unity was fulfilled by agreement on a platform. And the favored candidate was reassuringly presidential in stature. Under these conditions, the prejudices that a part of this electorate, which was repelled by Mélenchon's undemocratic practices and charismatic rhetoric (even when his discourse reflected their own convictions), could be overcome. And if this was so, I believe it was because the shock treatment— akin to a kick in the anthill— administered by the "great leader" applied well to a population that was committed to the program he presented to the nation, for it was precisely theirs. In the end, what appeared to be a logical contradiction— an undemocratic path to the construction of a democratic order—was transformed into its opposite once it encountered a social body, the left of the left, imbued with democratic convictions and carrying *revolutionary* aspirations.

Jean-Luc Mélenchon may well seem to have hijacked the inheritance for his own benefit. At the end of a skillfully conducted blitzkrieg within the NUPES, La France Insoumise took the lion's share of the constituencies to be filled in the legislative elections that shortly followed the presidential ones, thus securing the greatest number of seats in Parliament and thereby the territorial presence it had lacked, at the same time as its leader gained a lasting position as the official voice of the opposition to Macron. In any case, the predominant feeling—or at least the one expressed by the various parties involved—is that the successful unification of the left allowed it to correct its course and envisage a new future.

The left-right divide, which was said to be outdated, is back in full view, even though the split turns out to be extremely unequal, given the preponderance of the right and the rise of the far right. Despite its disagreements on the European Union[15] and on nuclear power,[16] the new Left, this time discernible as such, committed to a common program, seems well positioned to wage a common struggle. The activists emerging from this chaotic process are, more than in the recent past, clearly identifiable as representative of a rainbow of emancipation; a horizontal associative culture, concretely inserted as such within French society; a unionism with revolutionary traditions; and a radicalism that only the primacy given to environmentalism can bring. Thus, at the confluence of these various vectors, we can glimpse the possibility of another popular mode of practice and organization. If such a mutation were to occur, the emergence of this new generation, partly resulting from collective practices outside parties and movements, could appear as the start of a new cycle.

This electoral victory, coming at the end of social struggles that it continued to drive forward, has given left-wing elected representatives greater parliamentary capacity. But what impetus can it give to the popular movement? Clearly, a "representative body" has acquired pre-eminence in the political organization of the popular left for the next five years. We are reminded of the fears of the revolutionaries of yesteryear that parliamentary representatives take precedence over party leaders. Faced with the permanent danger of drifting into elitism, political leadership had to remain the task of those elected by their members for this purpose, according to the principle of democratic centralism. In principle, at least, one might say… We can certainly imagine that a mechanism for the "permanent revocability" of elected representatives could do better. However, such a mechanism only exists today on the drawing-board. Furthermore, in the current legislative process, the control the population can have over its representatives is weakened even more by the fact that they are often parachuted from above; as such, they are unknown locally and all the more inaccessible to their constituents. The body of elected representatives finds itself further empowered by the fact that they are the ones who appear first in the media, at the whim of the financial powers that control them, making the most of the best speakers. It is true that new institutions are being set up under promising but somewhat metaphorical names, such as "assemblies," "councils," or "parliaments." But here again, these are local or national emanations of the "representative body."

In short, it would appear that, for the time being, the popular left is very far from satisfying the four concerns designated above as the conditions of its practice: the unity of people A and people B, groundedness, the symbiosis of heterogeneous political identities, and insurance against the dangers of "competence." It is to be feared that part of the "victory" will once again elude the common people.

### *What Horizon in 2024?*

As the writing of this book was completed in July 2023, I cannot, in the continuity of this appendix devote to the case of France, shirk the need to extend it up to the most recent events, with a few remarks in reference to the hypotheses put forward in this book. Its translation into English, completed in June 2024, invites me to make a few further additions.

The situation does not call for optimism. Emmanuel Macron has managed to promulgate his pension reform law. Despite having only a relative majority in Parliament, he now seems to have the political means at his disposal to push forward, piecemeal, the essential elements of his neoliberal project. We can already see him pushing ahead, through a series of discreet measures, with the further privatization of education, health, transport, and housing; the criminalization of any union or environmental resistance; the refusal to welcome migrants; the repression of any demonstrations deemed hostile, etc. The union mobilization against the pension reform certainly demonstrated the existence of a solid and promising fabric of social solidarity among the salaried workers. But also its limits: In the absence of a parliamentary victory, the will of the people, even if it is in the majority, cannot "make the law."

The major contextual element seems to be the inexorable progression of far-right parties throughout Europe, to the point of threatening France itself. To maintain his ability to govern, Macron must ally himself with a *radical* right, which today presents strong affinities with the far right. The latter, hostile to all forms of taxation, and therefore indifferent to the fate of public services and social solidarity, can recognize itself in this project, consider participating in a neoliberal government, or even hope to take the lead. Indeed, it has already won an essential battle: if not that of ideas, at least that of their production and distribution. Emmanual Macron's handling of the urban revolts demonstrated the far right's influence today over the ruling bloc and public opinion, resulting in a racist, authoritarian ideology endorsed by the leaders of the parliamentary "right," driven by the police unions, and orchestrated by both private media empires—the meteoric rise of Vivendi is exemplary in this respect—and public media outlets. In the absence of any common interests between those who vote for the parties within this coalition, ranging from the Rassemblement National (Le Pen) to Renaissance (Macron), this seems to cement those who are opposed to the popular bloc. A left-wing alliance under popular hegemony must be formed against a right-wing alliance under the influence of the far right, but also under the hegemony of neoliberalism (and this remains essential). Immigration, a marginal phenomenon in the life of French society, can thus become a crucial element. The latest events confirm this.

In the 2023 "riots," as they were called, the rebels (*révoltés*)—those of the first hour, a few thousand people, but in whom millions more could recognize themselves—responded to the enactment of a death drive that targets them, to a social crime that insulted their lived experiences and family memories, and which typically bears the mark of the colonial contempt to which they were subjected. Paradoxically, their closest and most precious shared possessions were what they suddenly rejected first. All the more so as these things were familiar to them, as tangible parts of themselves, schools and recreation centers (paradoxical places of inclusion/exclusion), just as one comes, in a fit of anger, to pulverize the family dishes. Impotent rage. The whole prevailed over the parts: the whole of society, the whole of life, over the fragments of existence conceded. For the "rebels," the "happy days" had never come. They no longer accepted being discriminated against in recruitment, forgotten by the training and education programs that open the door to stable employment, subjected to the whims of administrative dependence day after day, forgotten by the media, invisible except to the police. These populations suffocate in the "state of nature" in which they have been confined, where the poor, the racialized, the disabled—who are also the most exploited—and single-parent families are crowded together in the same neighborhoods. The best equipped are the first to flee. The others gradually follow, as we know, due to the logic of gentrification. And public policies actively feed this logic by assigning the deprived to places to which, seen from above, they are predestined. In this general context, the revolts were a response to a policy of impoverishment driven by the powers that be, through the whole range of ministries occupied with the obscure and multifaceted task of recovering, according to a predefined percentage of savings, what had been granted to the poorest populations during the age of the "social state" in terms of access to housing, schools, hospitals, and even security, to a certain extent. All of this added together, the situation was a ticking time bomb.

We must therefore consider these revolts to be a social movement. But in what sense were they a political movement? The notion of "riots" amalgamates disparate elements. An examination of the sequence of the process reveals various practices. A scheme of ideal types can be put forward to distinguish three somewhat successive waves. First came the "*rebels*" (*révoltés*), those of the first hour. Then came the "*avant-gardists*," whose parasitic practices, as we have seen, graft themselves onto events in progress. They more willingly chose targets that represent capital, such as banks or luxury establishments. But just as political were, in their own way, the "workers of the last hour," the *looters*, who during the revolts came to recover what society had stolen from them. They particularly appreciate the signs of "distinction," whether brand-name clothing or high-tech devises, which are required to be part of the "middle class." It must be said that the political sentiment, in all of this, was without perspective. Yet, it could be that the revolts carried with them, as if in a negative way, the symptoms of a possible destiny.

We must nevertheless be careful not to draw ill-considered conclusions from this "flamboyant" episode. Some have called for a convergence between this urban movement and the environmental uprising. A convergence has indeed already taken place, as witnessed, in both cases, by the declarations and demonstrations of hundreds of associative, cultural, and political organizations declaring their solidarity and speaking out against the repression. But solidarity with the revolts does not have the same horizons as convergence with uprisings. *Alternative* urban policies—social policies, educational policies, urban planning, etc.—are the aim, of course, just as solidarity with uprisings aims for alternative environmental-protection policies. But the mode of concrete junction cannot be the same in these two cases. Environmental solidarity is a matter of common, conscious, and defined objectives, between the practices of uprising and those of political organizations. As for revolts, the lessons they teach can only emerge from the creative momentum of the people in rebellion, through the efflorescence of multiple cooperative, solidarity, and cultural initiatives that exist in marginalized neighborhoods, especially when they can be relayed within supportive municipal institutions. The neoliberal powers that be are doing their utmost to cut off supplies to this breeding ground for disturbing forces.

These forces must therefore rely first and foremost on themselves. This does not mean that we can repeat the refrain, "Only proletarians can liberate proletarians… Only women, etc." Through this associative and creative movement, the world of marginalized urban neighborhoods is actually linked to a broader social dynamic; it participates in the cultural vitality of the popular class as a whole, and therefore also in "big politics," if by this we mean that in which political organizations are engaged. But this cultural-political mix cannot take place without an economic mix that dissolves "diversity" in the common social space—i.e., without the popular conquest of equality.

As far as uprisings are concerned, I will be brief, since they were the topic of the final chapter of this book. In Marx's view, France was the classic site of modern political revolution, while England was carrying out an economic revolution, and Germany, a philosophical revolution. We can only dream that the same could be said of the "uprisings" that are now the driving force of the eco-socialist revolution. There are a few plausible reasons for this. In France—and this is almost an exception in Europe—there is a firmly established popular left in which the old revolutionary traditions, which seem to have almost disappeared in Italy, Germany, and elsewhere, have begun to pass the relay to innovative political organizations that firmly unite socialism, feminism, and environmentalism, to the point of committing themselves to a common platform along these lines. This capacity provides, at the very least, a favorable context for uprisings, which can only exist as such if they are based on a coherent overall vision, one that is jointly social, political, and ecological. The recent ban of Earth Uprisings (Soulèvements de la Terre) by the French government thus seems to signal a baptism of fire for a struggle as far as the eye can see, which no amount of repression will be able to "dissolve."

Two years after the last elections, a few new facts must be considered concerning the ongoing political recomposition of the popular left. Its four components, unequal but always identifiable, remain in place, although each of them is subject to strong tensions. Concerning La France Insoumise, we can see the contradiction inherent in Jean-Luc Mélenchon's enterprise—to achieve democratic objectives by non-democratic means—developing in a positive way: A plurality of internal groupings is emerging. The Parti de gauche (Left Party), which was the founding group of the movement, remains predominant in the background. But we must note the surprising resurfacing of its core precursor, the Parti ouvrier indépendant (POI, Independent Workers' Party), a member of the Fourth International within which Jean-Luc Mélenchon received his initial political training. Finally, an eco-socialist left has asserted itself, in particular affinity with Ensemble!, its precursor. Not to mention the appearance of symptomatic personalities, such as François Ruffin or Clémentine Autain, who could possibly take over from Jean-Luc Mélenchon. Everything suggests that, in each of the four components, developments will rapidly become clearer. But it is worth noting that the Greens are accentuating their left-wing orientation, as they demonstrated during the recent repressions of environmental uprisings and urban revolts; the growing legitimacy of the environmental struggle forces them to turn away from greenwashing.

The Socialists, who remained in the background during these events, seem to be resisting the strong pressure to withdraw from the game. Let's not forget that the rearguard is an essential part any great army, and it's important that it stands firm. As for the Communists, who today seem to be seeking their identity in their singularity, and their future in their past, they seem to have dropped out in some respects, sacrificing an essential part of their age-old potential for uprisings and internationalism; the influence of Communist activists has weakened accordingly. The most decisive factor, it seems to me, is the internal process within LFI, which heralds an inevitable transformation, but which yet provides no evidence of an impending implosion. For the time being, this development seems more likely to stimulate permeability between the various components of the NUPES. In parallel, the display of unity among labor unions, more impressive than that of the parliamentary coherence of the popular left during the battle against the pension reform, remains exemplary, even if it takes place in different territories.

The European Parliament elections held on June 9, 2024, which mixed up the political landscape in France and elsewhere, were a terrible challenge for the NUPES. The construction of a single, united list was undermined by divisions that especially concerned international issues, such as the relations between Europe and the United States, the Russian invasion of Ukraine, and the Israeli-Palestinian conflict. This pushed each party to distinguish itself from the others. Under these conditions, the spirit of unity was tarnished. The Socialist list, spearheaded by Raphaël Glucksmann, an emerging charismatic figure, shifted to the center and made notable progress, reaching 14%, the highest score among the parties that had formed the NUPES. The LFI list held its ground at 10%, while the traditionally pro-EU Green list struggled on its own turf, with a score of 5.5%. It is worth noting that such divisions over international issues are nothing new, and that this didn't prevent the *Programme commun* from emerging in the 1970s. For the time being, however, the perspective of unity may seem seriously impaired, while the "hard" right is increasingly fraternizing with the far right, which achieved the historic score of 37%. The unexpected dissolution of the National Assembly on the very evening of the election by Emmanuel Macron, unable to govern under these conditions, rang out like thunder. A new Popular Front (*Front populaire*) brought together not only the four founding members of the NUPES, but also all the major labor unions that had fought together against the labor and pension reform laws. This situation, unprecedented since 1936, gave rise to a powerful mobilization. Will the reinvigorated left prevail over far-right populism? At the time of writing, nothing is yet certain. The purpose of this reflection, however, is not to predict the future. It is to examine the present and seek the conditions for a better future.

## Notes

1 See, for example, *Propositions pour un plan de rupture*, (Plus jamais ça—Alliance écologique et sociale, 2021), https://alliance-ecologique-sociale.org/wp-content/uploads/2022/03/plan-de-rupture.pdf. This political

manifesto was signed by 16 trade unions and socioenvironmental associations. It was translated into practice in the program of the Nouvelle Union populaire écologique et sociale (NUPES, New Ecological and Social People's Union), an electoral alliance that included most of France's left-wing political parties during the French legislative elections of 2021.

2 This is notably the case in Aurélie Trouvé, *Le bloc arc-en-ciel: pour une stratégie politique radicale et inclusive* [The Rainbow Coalition: For a Radical and Inclusive Political Strategy] (Paris: La Découverte, 2021).

3 I owe readers a few clarifications on the political context in which I formulated these proposals. As a member of the FASE (Fédération pour une alternative sociale et écologique, in English: Federation for a Social and Environmental Alternative), which was founded in 2008, joined the Front de Gauche (Left Front) in 2011, and became Ensemble! (Together!) in 2013, I came to commit myself, in the aftermath of the 2012 presidential election, to a campaign for a unitary organization of the popular left. I first outlined the "collective model" in the press: Jacques Bidet, "L'esprit d'association entre égaux assure la confiance mutuelle," *L'Humanité*, July 13, 2012; Jacques Bidet, Jean-Michel Drevon, and Ramzig Keucheyan, "Pour des Associations Front de Gauche à la base," *Le Monde*, October 1, 2012; Jacques Bidet, "Le Front de Gauche doit devenir le 'tiers parti'," *Libération*, Juin 6, 2014. At the same time, at the beginning of 2014, I initiated a "Call for a New Departure of the Front de Gauche," with Jean-Numa Ducange and Razmig Keucheyan. More than 1,400 activists joined, including many well-known personalities in the ranks of the so-called radical left, including, significantly, Georges Séguy, the former general secretary of the CGT, the largest labor union in France at the time. Only members of La France Insoumise shunned this initiative.

4 Jacques Bidet, "Les leçons des gilets jaunes aux gilets rouges," Tribune, *Libération*, December 22, 2018, www.liberation.fr/debats/2018/12/22/la-lecon-des-gilets-jaunes-aux-gilets-rouges_1699024/.

5 Bidet, "Les leçons des gilets jaunes aux gilets rouges." For a detailed presentation of these arguments, see Jacques Bidet, *« Eux » et « nous »?: une alternative au populisme de gauche* ["Us" and "Them?": An Alternative to Left-Wing Populism] (Paris: Éditions Kimé, 2018).

6 See Manuel Cervera-Marzal, *Le populisme de gauche: sociologie de la France insoumise* [Left-wing Populism: The Sociology of La France Insoumise] (Paris: La Découverte, 2021). This sociological study is based on a three-year immersion in the France Insoumise network. Similar assessments can be found in the recent writings of the political scientist Rémi Lefebvre.

7 Jean-Luc Mélenchon, *L'Avenir en commun: le programme pour l'Union populaire* [The Future in Common: The Program of the People's Union] (Paris: Éditions du Seuil, 2021).

8 Cervera-Marzal, *Le populisme de gauche*, 197.
9 Mélenchon, *L'Avenir en commun*, 11.
10 Cervera-Marzal, *Le populisme de gauche*, 310.
11 Programme du Conseil national de la Résistance (Program of the National Resistance Council). See Bernard Friot, *Vaincre Macron* [Defeating Macron] (Paris: La Dispute, 2017).
12 See Alain Ruscio, *Les communistes et l'Algérie: des origines à la guerre d'indépendance, 1920–1962* [The Communists and Algeria: From the Origins to the War for Independence, 1920–1962] (Paris: La Découverte, 2019).
13 Parti communiste français and Parti socialiste (France), *Programme commun de gouvernement du Parti communiste français et du Parti socialiste (27 juin 1972)* [Common Government Program of the Communist Party and the Socialist Party] (Paris,: Éditions sociales, 1972).
14 This memorable event, attended by the author of these lines, brought together tens of thousands of political activists. Their fists raised high, *The Internationale* resonated. Mitterrand was the last to speak, greeting the participants, obviously drawn in close ranks from the "Red Belt": "You who come from Puteaux!… You who come from Saint-Denis!… From Levallois!…, etc." The incantation left the audience indifferent. After ten minutes, he came to pronounce the words "Programme commun." Frenzied applause. Then a heavy silence fell once again, until a few minutes later when the slogan "Programme commun" returned. Once again, frenzied excitement... Mitterand's repugnance to programmatic constraints had already manifested itself in the aftermath of 1968, when he seemed to respond to those for whom the "seizure of power" was immediately on the agenda.
15 This divide has less to do with the degree of attachment to Europe as a historical community, rich in social and political achievements that are the fruit of popular struggles shared between the various nations, than with the European Union's submission to neoliberalism.
16 The "nuclear question" is certainly a highly social and political one. It nevertheless presents an element of scientific appreciation. It separates those who see the possible diffusion of waste into the environment as the highest form of ecological risk, from those who consider the irreversible dangers posed by global warming to millions of living species to be incomparably greater, nuclear power representing an inescapable remedy, at least temporarily.

## References

Bidet, Jacques. *« Eux » et « nous »?: une alternative au populisme de gauche.* ["Us" and "Them?": An Alternative to Left-Wing Populism.] Paris: Éditions Kimé, 2018.

———. "L'esprit d'association entre égaux assure la confiance mutuelle." *L'Humanité*, July 13, 2012.

———. "Le Front de Gauche doit devenir le 'tiers parti'." *Libération*, Juin 6, 2014.

———. "Les leçons des gilets jaunes aux gilets rouges." Tribune, *Libération*, December 22, 2018. www.liberation.fr/debats/2018/12/22/la-lecon-des-gilets-jaunes-aux-gilets-rouges_1699024/.

Bidet, Jacques, Jean-Michel Drevon, and Ramzig Keucheyan. "Pour des Associations Front de Gauche à la base." *Le Monde*, October 1, 2012.

Cervera-Marzal, Manuel. *Le populisme de gauche: sociologie de la France insoumise.* [Left-wing Populism: The Sociology of La France Insoumise.] Paris: La Découverte, 2021.

Friot, Bernard. *Vaincre Macron.* [Defeating Macron.] Paris: La Dispute, 2017.

Mélenchon, Jean-Luc. *L'Avenir en commun: le programme pour l'Union populaire.* [The Future in Common: The Program of the People's Union.] Paris: Éditions du Seuil, 2021.

Parti communiste français, and Parti socialiste (France). *Programme commun de gouvernement du Parti communiste français et du Parti socialiste (27 juin 1972).* [Common Government Program of the Communist Party and the Socialist Party.] Paris,: Éditions sociales, 1972.

*Propositions pour un plan de rupture.* Plus jamais ça – Alliance écologique et sociale, 2021.

Ruscio, Alain. *Les communistes et l'Algérie: des origines à la guerre d'indépendance, 1920–1962.* [The Communists and Algeria: From the Origins to the War for Independence, 1920–1962.] Paris: La Découverte, 2019.

Trouvé, Aurélie. *Le bloc arc-en-ciel: pour une stratégie politique radicale et inclusive.* [The Rainbow Coalition: For a Radical and Inclusive Political Strategy.] Paris: La Découverte, 2021.

# Index

*Note*: Endnotes are indicated by the page number followed by "n" and the note number e.g., 111n5 refers to note 5 on page 111.

For Product Safety Concerns and Information please contact our EU representative GPSR@taylorandfrancis.com
Taylor & Francis Verlag GmbH, Kaufingerstraße 24, 80331 München, Germany

www.ingramcontent.com/pod-product-compliance
Lightning Source LLC
LaVergne TN
LVHW010923110826
845149LV00013B/2462

* 9 7 8 1 0 3 2 8 4 3 5 9 9 *